How Long, O Lord?

♦ Ralph E. Neall ♦

How Long, O Lord?

Review and Herald Publishing Association
Washington, DC 20039-0555
Hagerstown, MD 21740

Copyright © 1988 by
Review and Herald Publishing Association

This book was
Edited by Gerald Wheeler
Designed by Dennis Ferree
Cover design by Bill Kirstein

Printed in U.S.A.

Bible texts in this book credited to RSV are from the Revised Standard Version of the Bible, copyright 1946, 1952 © 1971, 1973.

Library of Congress Cataloging in Publication Data

Neall, Ralph E., 1927-
  How long, O Lord?/Ralph E. Neall.
    p.   cm.
  Bibliography: p.

  1. Second Advent—History of doctrines—19th century. 2. White, Ellen Gould Harmon, 1827-1915. 3. Seventh-day Adventists—Doctrines—History—19th century. 4. Adventists—Doctrines—History—19th century. I. Title.
BX6154.N4 1988
236'.9—dc19   87-25957
                                                                                CIP

ISBN 0-8280-0399-8

Contents

Introduction	7
Background of the Millerite Movement	17
Ellen Harmon in the Millerite Movement	22
The Nearness of Christ's Coming	40
The Delay of Christ's Coming	87
The Two Streams Merge	118
How Then Should We Live? The Bible Answer	127
Appendix	132
Bibliography	148

INTRODUCTION

The Advent Movement 14 Decades Later

The year was 1944, the scene a dormitory room in Union Springs Academy. My roommate and I were polishing our shoes after a 13-hour day of Medical Cadet Corps classes and drills. Not quite old enough to be drafted, we were still getting ready. We had no way of knowing how long the war would last.

"George," I asked my friend, "you read the war news. You see the mess the world is in. How long do you think it will be before Jesus comes?"

"I don't know, Ralph," he replied, "but I should think the final events could all happen in five years. I don't see how time could last beyond 1950."

I agreed, wondering if time would last even that long. It seemed as though all the signs of the times had appeared, except for the very final ones. We wondered whether we would get to college, and dreams of marriage and family seemed impossible.

My father later told me he had felt the same way in 1917, during the First World War. He never expected to live long enough to marry and have children. I was glad he did, however!

But now four decades have passed since that day in the dormitory, and seven decades since my father's experience. Time has gone on much longer than we expected. While I still believe Jesus is coming soon, I am now wondering, How soon is soon? How near is near? What

HOW LONG, O LORD?

did Jesus mean when He said, "Behold, I come quickly"? So many dates have been set, but all have passed.

The question is not new, of course. Believers have been asking it ever since God promised He would send His Son to crush the serpent's head under His feet. Adam and Eve hoped their firstborn might be the Deliverer, but the fulfillment of the promise tarried.[1] Century after century God's spokesmen repeated the word, but He came not.

The psalmist voiced the universal longing for deliverance. In Psalm 74:9, 10 we read, "We do not see our signs; there is no longer any prophet, and there is none among us who knows how long. How long, O God, is the foe to scoff? Is the enemy to revile thy name for ever?" (RSV). And in Psalm 94:1-3 we hear the plea, "O Lord, thou God of vengeance, thou God of vengeance, shine forth! Rise up, O judge of the earth; render to the proud their deserts! O Lord, how long shall the wicked, how long shall the wicked exult?" (RSV). Habakkuk voiced the same cry (Hab. 1:1-4), and the Lord told him that the vision would "surely come, it will not delay" (Hab. 2:3, RSV). But it seemed to delay for many generations. Every one who believes in a just and loving God asks the question "How long?"

Christ's appearance had no real delay, however. God's plan was fulfilled on schedule. In her chapter "The Fullness of Time," Ellen White in *The Desire of Ages* referred to Daniel 9:24-27 and observed,

> Like the stars in the vast circuit of their appointed path, God's purposes know no haste and no delay. . . . So in heaven's council the hour for the coming of Christ had been determined. When the great clock of time pointed to that hour, Jesus was born in Bethlehem.[2]

Not many understood, however, and when Jesus was born, only the shepherds and the Wise Men expected

INTRODUCTION

Him. Everyone else kept on asking, "How long?"

In the Babylonian Talmud,[3] put into writing several hundred years after Christ, we find speculations about why the Messiah had not come yet. Some rabbis believed the world would last 6,000 years, with the world lying desolate during the seventh thousand, but in discouragement they wrote that through their iniquities all the past years were lost. One school set the date A.D. 240. Their answer to why the Messiah had not arrived was that the time had not come. Another school renounced all efforts to reckon the date, saying "Blasted be the bones of those who calculate the end. For they would say, since the predetermined time has arrived, and yet he has not come, he will never come. But [even so] wait for him, as it is written, though he tarry, wait for him." Some said that since the predestined dates had passed, the matter now "depends only on repentance and good deeds." The Messiah would arrive when all Israel should have repented. Others concluded that the kingdom would come only when the number of elect was complete. Finally, some suggested that the Son of David would not appear until the whole world had converted to the belief of the heretics (referring to the conversion of Rome to Christianity under Constantine).

Even those who accepted Christ as the Promised One had to admit that He had not fulfilled all the prophecies. He had come as a meek and suffering servant, but not as a conquering king. Although He had healed the sick and raised a few of the dead, when would He raise them all? The disciples raised the question just before Jesus returned to heaven: "Lord, will you at this time restore the kingdom to Israel?" (Acts 1:6, RSV).

"It is not for you to know times or seasons which the Father has fixed by his own authority," He answered, "but you shall receive power when the Holy Spirit has come upon you; and you shall be my witnesses . . . to the end of the earth" (verse 7, RSV). It is not for you to know—but you shall be My witnesses. You are to do My work, and leave the times and seasons with God.

One would expect His words to prevent Christian speculations about the end, but they have not. The book of Revelation indeed says, "The time is near" and "Surely I am coming soon," (Rev. 1:3; 22:20, RSV). But it also says, "You will not know at what hour I will come upon you" (Rev. 3:3, RSV). Even so, these verses have not prevented Christians from trying to calculate the end.

A group known as Montanists expected the Lord to return in the year set by some of the rabbis: A.D. 240. Two women among them claimed to have the gift of prophecy, and their lifestyle was similar to that of early Adventists as they waited for the end. Joachim of Fiore thought 1260 would usher in the age of the Spirit. The Puritans looked to 1660. Jonathan Edwards conjectured that the Lord might arrive in 1739. Finally William Miller set the date 1844, and date-setters exist even today.

What attitude shall we take toward such speculations? What does an Adventist say 14 decades later, as the years keep marching on? But before we consider Adventist answers, we will take a quick look at other views widespread in the world today.

Many conservative Christians believe that the establishment of the nation of Israel in 1948 was the key sign of the end, and therefore Christ can now appear at any time. They say His coming will occur in two stages, known as the "rapture" and the "revelation," seven years apart. During those seven years chapters 4 to 19 of the book of Revelation will be fulfilled consecutively. That is to say, the trumpets will follow the seven seals, then the beasts, and the plagues in order. The "rapture" refers to the unannounced coming of Christ for Christians, and the "revelation" to His return in the clouds to deal with Jews and everyone else. During the millennium He will reign

INTRODUCTION

over the earth from a literal throne in Jerusalem, with converted Jews as officers of His government. Most of the world will accept God, for the devil will be bound and unable to tempt them. Only a small remnant of wicked will remain to attack His holy city at the end of the thousand years.

Because the teaching puts most of the prophecies of Revelation after the rapture, it is known as "futurism." In this system of interpretation, the book of Revelation offers information about the future that is irrelevant to Christians, because they expect God to remove them before He fulfills the prophecies. The best-known futurist writer today is Hal Lindsey, author of the best-selling *The Late Great Planet Earth*. One can criticize the doctrine on the grounds that it holds out a second chance if one is not raptured. It also makes a sharp distinction between Jews and Christians, with an earthly reward for the former and a heavenly for the latter.

Liberal Christianity, on the other hand, commonly believes that the book of Revelation had its fulfillment in the days of John himself. Its only value for today lies in its exhortations to be faithful under persecution, and in its confidence that God is sovereign over the affairs of earth. Known as "preterism," this view, like futurism, also removes the prophecies from any present application.[4]

Futurism answers the question of the delayed Advent by making it contingent on the return of the Jews to Palestine. Since they did resettle the land four decades ago, Christians now live in an any-moment expectancy. No other condition needs to be met now. Preterism, on the other hand, avoids the question of the delayed Advent by denying the coming of Christ completely.

Not all modern scholars follow either the futurist or the preterist systems of interpretation. There are conservatives who are not futurists and liberals who are not preterists. During the past century many have given a great deal of thought to the supposed delay of Christ's return.

Albert Schweitzer, for instance, concluded that Jesus believed the kingdom of heaven would arrive by harvesttime in the same year He spoke. He saw Jesus predicting His own glorious coming in Matthew 10:23—"You will not have gone through all the towns of Israel, before the Son of man comes." But, Schweitzer said, Christ was wrong.[5] His view is known as "consistent eschatology." Schweitzer's achievement was that he forced scholars to take the New Testament promises seriously. One could not abstract them from the text without destroying its original intentions. But Schweitzer's weakness was that He disbelieved the predictions of Christ Himself.

Thirty years later C. H. Dodd defended Christ by blaming the church. Statements describing a literal Second Advent did not originate from Christ, Dodd said. Instead the early church put them in His mouth. Dodd decided from his studies of the Gospel of John and the parables that the Second Advent was merely Christ's coming to each individual at his conversion,[6] a view known as "realized eschatology." He emphasized the present blessings of Christians and demonstrated that verses such as John 14:18 and 23 clearly refer to a present spiritual coming of Christ to the believer. But his weakness was that he credited all the evidence for a future literal Advent to the church instead of Christ.

Rudolf Bultmann interpreted the second advent of Christ in existential terms. He said that the predictions of the kingdom tell us simply that Christ confronts every man in each moment of decision. Christ continually calls us to better things.[7] His view is a later version of Dodd's.

Oscar Cullmann took a much more conservative view. Employing an illustration from World War II, he wrote that the cross was D-Day and the Second Coming will be V-Day. In other words, God fought the decisive battle at

INTRODUCTION

the cross. The Lord is now engaged in mopping-up operations, and the final victory will occur momentarily. The issues have been settled, so the outcome is not in doubt.[8] Cullman's view takes all the biblical evidence seriously, but fails to explain why the mopping-up should take so long.

These are the major attempts modern scholars have made to explain the apparently delayed Advent. None can say they have not faced the problem seriously. Adventists think of a delay since 1844, while non-Adventists see a delay since the first advent of Christ. For them the problem is more serious than for us, but the lengthening decades are increasing it for us also. The delayed Advent was a problem for both Israel and the church, and it remains so today. Indeed, we could fairly say that the delayed Advent is the greatest problem of all Christian theology. None of the suggestions we have reviewed would have been necessary if Jesus had come!

We turn back now to the Adventist answers to the delay. In the beginning five major responses arose to the great disappointment of October 22, 1844.

First, the date-setters kept extending the time. Some looked to October 22, 1845. Joseph Bates predicted the Lord would come in 1851. He reasoned that the high priest sprinkled the blood seven times on the mercy seat in the earthly sanctuary, and each spot could stand for one year. Ellen White, however, warned the believers that all such dates would pass, for the third angel's message would never hang on time again.

Second, some gave up their faith completely, even to denying the existence of God. Others retained their faith in God, but said they had been deluded in thinking that anything special was to happen in 1844. Most joined other churches.

Third, a number claimed that prophecy had indeed been fulfilled in 1844. The Lord had come, but in a

HOW LONG, O LORD?

spiritual manner. Their position reminds us of the belief of C. H. Dodd.

Fourth, a remnant grew into our own church. They retained William Miller's prediction of a judgment to begin in 1844, but believed it was a *pre*-Advent judgment in heaven, not an *Advent* judgment on earth.

Finally, Miller himself said that he was resolved to expect the Lord today! and Today! and TODAY! until He finally appears.[9] Miller's reaction is similar to that of the futurists' any-moment expectancy.

Now, in the late twentieth century, Adventists offer four other responses to the problem of the delay. First are the chartmakers and date-setters, who disagree on details but agree that all the prophecies of Daniel and Revelation will have a second fulfillment in the future, with the periods now marked by literal rather than prophetic time. Many feel that the Lord will surely come before the year 2000 because the world cannot last more than 6,000 years. If one took Archbishop Ussher's dates that were printed in the old King James Bible seriously, the year 2000 would be close to the 6,000th year of the earth.

At the other extreme are those who are losing their faith. Saying, "My Lord delayeth His coming," they are beginning to eat and drink with the drunken. With the future dim in their minds, they live for the present.

Third, we find those who believe that Christ will return, but are no longer sure we can know anything about the time, pointing out that regardless of when Jesus comes, no one's probation can last longer than his own lifetime.[10] Perhaps this is why no one has picked up the pen of Arthur Maxwell, who used to write a book every year on the coming of Christ. We do not hear sermons on the Advent as often as we used to. It is a strange paradox that now, when the world stares into an atomic abyss, we Adventists have so little to say about our hope of a new world.

INTRODUCTION

The majority position of the church is that Jesus is indeed coming soon, but that our failure to live holy lives and preach the gospel to the world have postponed His coming. This view says that Christ will come just as soon as the harvest is ripe, a conviction well summarized in the eloquent appeals of the Autumn Councils of 1973 and 1974,[11] and later detailed in Herbert Douglass's book *The End: Unique Voice of Adventists About the Return of Jesus*, (Mountain View, Calif.: Pacific Press Pub. Assn., 1979).

What should be our stance during the last decades of the twentieth century? Are our failures the only reason that Jesus has not come? How long can we go on saying this? How can we avoid setting dates on one hand or losing our faith on the other? Is there a prophetic voice to guide us now?

When Ellen White was alive, Seventh-day Adventists looked to her for answers to such questions. If only she were alive today! What guidance she could offer in our puzzling, frantic, but thrilling times! The Lord did not leave us alone, however. The Holy Spirit still leads. We still have our Bibles, and we still have Ellen White's writings. Here are principles just as valid as when first written.

We need to trace them out and apply them to our questions today, a task similar to that of a firing officer who computes the trajectory of his missile. Knowing the weight of the missile, the thrust of its rocket, and its altitude and direction, he can predict where it will impact.

Here is our goal in this book. We shall look at Ellen Harmon's experience in the Millerite movement as the foundation of her entire eschatology (eschatology means the study of last-day events). We will examine her statements on the delay and the nearness of Christ's coming, investigate how she used eschatology in her exhortations, and then try to extend them into our own day. In other words, we will plot the trajectory of her thought, trying to

HOW LONG, O LORD?

determine what she would say if she were alive now.

FOOTNOTES

[1] *The Desire of Ages*, p. 31.

[2] *Ibid.*, p. 32.

[3] In the volume *Sanhedrin* (London: Soncino Press, 1935), pp. 97a, 97b. See also Oscar Cullmann, *Christ and Time* (London: SCM Press, Ltd., 1951), pp. 159, 160, for other sources. Among all the answers proposed today as to why Christ has not come back, few do not already appear in the ancient Jewish sources.

[4] As a matter of fact, this is the reason that two Jesuits developed the two systems in the sixteenth century. Luis de Alcazar (1554-1613) was the author of preterism, and Francisco Ribera (1537-1591) of futurism. Their motives seem to have been to turn the prophetic spotlight away from the papacy, which the Protestant Reformers condemned as the scriptural antichrist. See Leroy Edwin Froom, *The Prophetic Faith of Our Fathers* (Washington, D.C.: Review and Herald Pub. Assn., 1948), vol. 2, pp. 507-509 and pp. 489-493.

[5] Albert Schweitzer, *The Quest of the Historical Jesus* (New York: Macmillan, 1961), pp. 358, 360, 370, 371.

[6] C. H. Dodd, *The Parables of the Kingdom*, rev. ed. (New York: Charles Scribner's Sons, 1961), pp. 43, 44, 57, 61, 77, 81, 100, 103.

[7] Rudolf Bultmann, "New Testament and Mythology," *Kerygma and Myth*, ed. H. W. Bartsch (New York: Harper and Row, Harper Torchbooks, 1961), pp. 1ff.

[8] Oscar Cullmann, *Christ and Time; The Primitive Christian Conception of Time and History*, 3rd ed. (London: SCM, 1962), pp. 84, 140-142.

[9] William Miller letter, Nov. 10, 1844, *The Midnight Cry*, Dec. 5, 1844.

[10] See the excellent articles on eschatology in *Spectrum*, September 1976.

[11] Reported in the *Review and Herald*, Nov. 15 and Dec. 6, 1973, and Nov. 14, 1974.

CHAPTER I

Background of the Millerite Movement

The belief in the literal return of Jesus traces back to His own promises. He is the source of the stream that nourishes every believer's hope today. Wherever we begin our survey, we are dipping into a living stream from which many have drunk before us.

William Miller himself, although claiming to study nothing but the Bible and *Cruden's Concordance*, proclaimed a faith well known in his time. The advent faith was a legacy from the Puritans who brought it from England.

John Milton (1608-1674), who wrote *Paradise Lost*, believed that Christ would come and raise the dead before the millennium. Richard Baxter (1615-1691), a one-time army chaplain to Charles II, expressed his faith in vivid military terms:

> I have thought on it many a time, as a small emblem of that day, when I have seen a prevailing army drawing toward the towns and castles of the enemy: Oh, with what glad hearts do all the poor prisoners within hear the news, and behold our approach? How do they run up to their prison windows, and thence behold us with joy? How glad are they at the roaring report of that cannon, which is the enemies' terror? How do they clap each other on the back, and cry Deliverance, deliverance! . . .
>
> Fellow Christian, what a day will that be, when we who have been kept prisoners by sin, by sinners, by the grave, shall be fetch't out by the Lord Himself.[1]

HOW LONG, O LORD?

The Puritans believed that the prophecies of Daniel and Revelation were fulfilled in history although they were aware of other views. The Spanish Jesuit Luis de Alcazar (1554-1613) had recently proposed the preterist interpretation of Revelation, which applied the prophecies to John's own day. Another Jesuit, Francisco Ribera (1537-1591), had just proposed the futurist view, but the Puritans maintained that the papacy was the antichrist and the prophecies were meeting their fulfillment in their own day.

A child of the Puritans in the following century was Jonathan Edwards (1703-1758), who deserves more attention than he has received from Adventist writers. Admittedly, he introduced postmillennialism to America, and the postmillennialists became the harshest critics of William Miller. (Postmillennialism says the world will gradually improve with a thousand years of peace before Jesus returns. Premillennialism says the world will get worse before Christ returns, and the millennium will follow His advent.) But Edwards was a historicist in his interpretation of Revelation. He preached a series of sermons in 1739 that his son later published in a book entitled *A History of the Work of Redemption, Containing the Outline of a Body of Divinity in a Method Entirely New*.[2] In it Edwards traced the struggle between God and Satan and said God will eventually destroy the devil and restore all that sin had ruined.

Edwards shared many concepts with the premillennialists of his time. The red dragon of Revelation 12 was the Roman Empire, and the antichrist who received his seat from the dragon was the papacy. Using the day-for-a-year principle, he saw the 1260 years of Revelation 12 stretching from A.D. 479 to 1739 (when he was preaching his sermons). Few of the foretold signs of the times, he felt, remained to occur before "the beginning of the great work of God." He saw their manifestation in the preaching of the gospel to the American Indians, and in the Great

BACKGROUND OF THE MILLERITE MOVEMENT

Awakening started by George Whitefield in 1735. His book became extremely popular in the nineteenth century among those interested in Bible prophecies, helping to plow the soil in which the Millerite seeds grew.

The Second Great Awakening, which began in the last decade of the eighteenth century, also helped prepare the way for William Miller's ministry. In the East it centered in the colleges and towns along the coast. In the West people gathered in great camp meetings on the frontier, sometimes marked by religious excitement and emotional outbursts. The Millerites also later successfully used camp meetings to spread the news of Christ's coming.

The religious revival inspired a great multitude of voluntary associations. Societies formed for home and foreign missions, for distributing Bibles, for Sunday schools, for temperance, for freeing the slaves, for women's rights, and for education, diet, and health, and prison reform, to name a few.

Many of these goals later became part of the mission of the Seventh-day Adventist Church, but that was after the death of William Miller. Those who expected the Lord to come in just two or three years had no time for such programs.

Miller, like Jonathan Edwards before him, believed that he saw the signs of the times being fulfilled in his own time. He cited the preaching of the gospel, the pouring out of the Holy Spirit, the growth in religious knowledge, the increase of riches, scoffers, perilous times, and false teachers. Even the voluntary societies that marked the Second Great Awakening he viewed as an indication of the end, for they prepared the way for the "midnight cry" of the parable of the ten virgins.[3]

Such signs had appeared in every generation, of course, but Miller tied them to the time prophecies which all focused on his time, not only the 2300 days of Daniel 8, but also the 1260 days of Daniel 7, and the 1290 days and

HOW LONG, O LORD?

1335 days of Daniel 12. His coworker, Josiah Litch, predicted that Turkey would lose her sovereignty on August 11, 1840, on the basis of Revelation 9. His interpretation, published 10 days beforehand, added new credibility to Miller's principles and gained enormous new interest for his Advent belief.[4]

Miller's key text was Daniel 8:14—"Unto two thousand and three hundred days; then shall the sanctuary be cleansed." Believing that the "sanctuary" referred to the church and the earth, he concluded that God would cleanse the church and burn the world at the end of the 2300 days. In the early years of his preaching, Miller hesitated to set a date closer than "about the year 1843," but on January 1, 1843, he narrowed the prediction down to "between March 21, 1843, and March 21, 1844, according to the Jewish mode of computation of time."[5]

Surprisingly, Miller did not believe that the darkening of the sun and the falling of the stars in Matthew 24 were literal. For him the sun represented the light of the gospel extinguished in the early church, and the falling of the stars referred to ministers plunging into anti-Christian abominations.[6] It was his colleagues who applied the prediction to the dark day of May 19, 1780, and the star shower of November 13, 1833.[7]

Miller's followers set various dates during the years 1843 and 1844, but none gained wide acceptance until Samuel S. Snow suggested that the Lord would come on the day of atonement, the tenth day of the seventh month, which was October 22, 1844, according to Karaite Jewish reckoning. His date gained almost universal support, with Miller himself accepting it a few weeks before the expected end.

The zeal of the Millerites, their concern for sinners, their investment of means, their wise use of the press, their mammoth camp meetings—all together moved the country and turned thousands to the Advent hope. Some,

BACKGROUND OF THE MILLERITE MOVEMENT

including the Harmon family, of Portland, Maine, it changed forever.

FOOTNOTES

[1] Richard Baxter, *The Saints' Everlasting Rest, or, a Treatise of the Blessed State of the Saints in Their Enjoyment of God in Glory* (London: Thomas Underhill and Francis Taylor, 1652), pp. 49, 47.
[2] Published in New York by Shepard Kollock, for Robert Hodge, 1786.
[3] William Miller, *Evidence From Scripture and History* (Troy, N.Y.: Elias Gates, 1838), pp. 238-240.
[4] Josiah Litch, "Fall of the Ottoman Power in Constantinople; The End of the Second Woe," Rev. ix, *Signs of the Times of the Second Coming of Christ* (Boston), Aug. 1, 1840, p. 70.
[5] "Synopsis of Miller's Views," *Signs of the Times and Expositor of Prophecy*, Jan. 25, 1843, p. 147.
[6] Miller, *A Familiar Exposition of the Twenty-fourth Chapter of Matthew and the Fifth and Sixth Chapters of Hosea, to Which Are Added an Address to the General Conference on the Advent, and a Scene of the Last Day* (Boston: Joshua V. Himes, 1842), p. 25.
[7] See articles in *Signs of the Times and Expositor of Prophecy*: Josiah Litch, Sept. 7, 1842, p. 142; Joel Spaulding, Sept. 14, 1842, pp. 184-187; and Sylvester Bliss, Nov. 9, 1842.

CHAPTER II

Ellen Harmon in the Millerite Movement

Her Conversion

Born into a Methodist family, Ellen Harmon (1827-1915) was converted in 1840 at a Methodist camp meeting in Buxton, Maine, about the same time her family first heard William Miller lecturing in Portland. She longed for complete sanctification and holiness of heart, but for some time remained terrified that she was not ready for the coming of Christ. Eventually, after much prayer, she felt she had achieved entire conformity to the will of God. But since she credited her spiritual victory not to Methodism but to her hope in the imminent coming of Christ, she encountered severe opposition, and the Methodist church disfellowshipped her and her family in September 1843.[1]

The Harmons attended the Adventist meetings in Portland quite regularly. The time seemed so short that Ellen resolved to do all she could to lead sinners to Christ. Earning 25 cents a day knitting stockings and making hats, she spent it buying books and tracts to give away. Each page seemed to her to be a messenger of light to the world, bidding people prepare for the great event near at hand. Ellen carried a heavy burden for her young friends and arranged meetings with them. Several entire nights she prayed for them. Eventually all but one were converted to God.

When Jesus did not appear on the expected day in

ELLEN HARMON IN THE MILLERITE MOVEMENT

1844, Ellen Harmon endured the great disappointment with the rest, but unlike most she did not give up her faith that prophecy had been fulfilled. Her first vision, received a few weeks later, confirmed God's leading in the Millerite revival, although it did not yet offer any explanation for the disappointment.

The Structure of Ellen White's Eschatology

Ellen White believed with William Miller that the return of Christ in glory is the very keynote of the Sacred Scriptures, longed for by the children of faith ever since the fall in Eden. At His advent Christ will complete the great work of redemption. As with the shepherds in Bethlehem, the proclamation of His coming is "good tidings of great joy" because He who is our hope of eternal life will return in power and glory to redeem His people.

She later wrote that one of the purposes of Christ's second advent is to reap the harvest of the earth. It will be the end of the present age, the final judgment.

This judgment, however, involves much more than a mere courtroom scene. It is the climax of Ellen White's theodicy—her defense of the ways of God to men. The earth is a lesson book for intelligent beings throughout the universe, she wrote, and the issues being worked out here have ramifications far wider than the human race—issues that must be settled before God can allot the final rewards to men. We must consider them if we would understand her eschatology.[2]

Lucifer, the covering cherub in heaven before the creation of our world, rebelled against God's government and raised fundamental questions about His character and law. Impeaching His wisdom and love, Lucifer charged that God was a tyrant who imposed arbitrary laws on the angels, holy beings who needed no such control. Lucifer claimed that the law of God must be either changed or abrogated in order to bring true happiness in heaven. He said justice was inconsistent with mercy. Created beings could not obey the law, and when they didn't, God could not forgive them. Man's disobedience proved his point, he said, and thus he claimed the human race as his rightful subjects.

The law in Mrs. White's presentation includes more than the Ten Commandments, or even the five books of Moses. It stands for the sovereignty of God Himself. When Lucifer attacked the law, he was assailing the very government of the universe.

If God had destroyed Lucifer before he had a chance to work out his principles, the surviving angels would have served Him from fear, sowing the seeds for further rebellion. Since God desired the service of love, He had to deal with the rebellion in such a way that the universe could clearly see His goodness and the evil of sin. Only as He answered Satan's charges to the satisfaction of all could He place His government on a basis of eternal security.

Mrs. White wrote that the life and death of Christ refuted Satan's charges. The cross fully revealed the characters of both Satan and Christ. By His perfect life Jesus proved that the law is righteous and can be obeyed, while by His death He showed that the law is unalterable, for if it could have been changed, He need not have died. He upheld its authority while providing a way to forgive the sinner. God could therefore be just and the justifier of him who believes in Jesus.[3]

Ellen White believed that Christ can remit sin because His life stands for that of all men. He offers His holiness and perfection as a free gift to all who will receive it. "More than this, Christ imbues men with the attributes of God. He builds up the human character after the similitude of the divine character." Through the forgiveness of past sin and power against present sin, "the very righteousness of the law is fulfilled in the believer in Christ."[4] Thus He reconciles mercy and justice.

ELLEN HARMON IN THE MILLERITE MOVEMENT

Nevertheless, the controversy could not yet end even at the cross. The issues at stake must be more fully disclosed. Men as well as angels must see the characters of Christ and of Satan and choose the side on which they will stand.

After the resurrection of Christ, Mrs. White said, Satan attacked the law from a new standpoint. He declared that the death of Christ abrogated it. Mercy had destroyed justice. This will be the issue in the final crisis, when, under the pressure of persecution and threatened death, every man will have to decide whether he will obey God's law or man's.

Satan did not need to attack the entire law of God. He could gain his purpose by destroying one command, for that would eventually lead to disrespect for all. The particular target of his effort is the Sabbath commandment. To prepare the way for his final deception, Satan has led men to question the doctrines of Creation, the Fall of man, the atonement, and the authority of the Bible itself. The result is modern intemperance, corrupt courts, and increase in violent crime.

Throughout the struggle between good and evil, Ellen White taught, God has acted so as to bring men and angels to acknowledge His justice. He desires that they see Him as wise, just, and loving. After his final attack on God at the end of the millennium, even Satan will be brought to acknowledge God's goodness and the justice of his own sentence. Then God will have answered every question, and He will stand clear of blame for evil.

Then, in Mrs. White's view, "God will vindicate His law and deliver His people" by cutting off Satan and all who have joined him in rebellion. Because of the long continuance of evil, the righteous have asked in the words of Revelation 6:10—"How long . . . dost thou not judge and avenge our blood?"—a question that shows that God Himself needs to be vindicated before the righteous. Their doubts and questions will be satisfied at last. The extermination of sin will vindicate His love and establish His honor before the universe.

God's ultimate goal is a clean universe. While Christ has paid the redemption price for all and brought hope and salvation to the world, it is not yet fully realized. The cross is the pledge of everlasting life. At His coming Christ will bring everything to completion. Sin will be no more and He will create new heavens and a new earth as the eternal home of His people.

The Manner of Christ's Coming

Ellen White taught that Christ will return literally, personally, and visibly. He will arrive in the same manner as He went away. Men will see Him return just as they watched Him go. He will come in the glory of the Father, accompanied by all the angels. His second advent will be just as literal as His appearance on Sinai or His death on Calvary. For the righteous it will mean deliverance, resurrection, and translation. The final vindication of God's authority requires His personal intervention at the end of history.

Mrs. White insisted that these events will be literal and that just before the end Satan will counterfeit Christ's coming, but God will not allow him to imitate His appearance in glory. Only by knowing the biblical descriptions of the event will God's people be able to distinguish the true from the false.

The Sequence of Last-day Events

Ellen White accepted William Miller's predictions based on the prophecy of Daniel 8 and 9. Connecting the 70-week prophecy of Daniel 9 with the 2300-day prophecy of Daniel 8:14, she agreed with the 1844 date for the cleansing of the sanctuary and the return of Christ.

When the disciples went out to preach, "The time is

fulfilled, and the kingdom of God is at hand: repent ye, and believe the gospel," they based their message, Mrs. White wrote, on the prophecy of Daniel 9. Both Miller and the disciples were right about the time but wrong about the event, because both expected the kingdom of glory. The disciples did not see that Daniel 9 foretold the death of the Messiah, not His enthronement; and Miller did not understand that the sanctuary of Daniel 8:14 was in heaven, not on earth. Neither did he recognize that two other angels followed the first angel of Revelation 14:6, 7.

Because the disciples anticipated an earthly empire, Mrs. White explained, they thought they were proclaiming Christ's kingdom of glory, whereas the prophecy actually referred to His kingdom of grace. In a similar way, because the Millerites accepted the current idea that the sanctuary meant the earth, they assumed that Christ was about to return for final judgment. Both were wrong because they accepted popular errors, yet God accomplished His purpose in permitting the messages to be given the way they were.

In Mrs. White's presentation of the prophecies, Daniel 7-9 reveals the beginning of the "time of the end." She combined those prophecies with 2 Thessalonians 2, in which Paul warned the early church not to look for the coming of Christ in their day, for the man of sin must be revealed first. The little horn of Daniel 7 and the man of sin in 2 Thessalonians 2 both point to the papacy, and the time, times, and half a time of Daniel 7:25 extended to A.D. 1798. Since Paul "covers with his caution the whole of the Christian dispensation down to the year 1798," Christ could not come until after that year.[5]

She spoke repeatedly of living in the last days.[6] Quoting Revelation 10:5, 6 ("There should be time no longer"), she stated that no more time prophecies would follow the end of the 2300-day prophecy in 1844.[7] This concept is tremendously important in understanding her eschatology. While spelling it out most clearly on page 356 of *The Great Controversy*, she made it basic to the whole plan of the book. In it she gives an overview of church history, but only as a preparation for the final period. In the time of the end, life has a different quality and a greater urgency, with privileges and obligations beyond those of previous ages. Unlike Schweitzer and other modern eschatologists, she did not concern herself with an eighteen-century delay in Christ's coming. For her, "delay" referred only to the period after 1798 or 1844.[8]

Up to this point Mrs. White agreed with William Miller, but differed from him in the event of 1844 and in the prophecies to be fulfilled afterward. Like the early Christians, who divided the Old Testament expectation of the Messiah into two phases, she separated Miller's judgment into two parts, investigative and executive.

She said that the Millerite movement itself fulfilled the first two angels' messages of Revelation 14:6-8. The first predicted judgment focused on October 22, 1844. But she departed from Miller in accepting the new concept of the sanctuary suggested by Hiram Edson (1806-1882), who said that instead of Christ returning to earth on October 22, He then entered the Most Holy Place of the heavenly sanctuary for judgment. There He began to examine the heavenly records and blot out the sins of the repentant. When finished, she wrote, He will return to receive His people and make an end of sin on earth. Through such concepts she explained the Great Disappointment and also lent special urgency to the years afterward. The judgment was in session and no one could know when it might consider his name or when the task would be finished.

The second angel's message, Mrs. White agreed, applied to the Millerites being driven out of their churches in the summer of 1843. Charles Fitch's sermon, "'Come Out of Her, My People,'" made this application. She did not believe the churches were completely fallen, however, for in 1888 she described the future "loud cry" that would repeat the message of Revelation 14:8, and she mentioned corruptions that had entered the churches *since* 1844.[9]

The third angel's message with its emphasis on seventh-day Sabbath reform came to the believers' attention between 1846 and 1849. The beast of Revelation 14:9 represented the papacy. The image of the beast symbolized a future union between Protestant churches and American government that will seek to enforce religious laws by civil power. The mark of the beast will be a future national Sunday law, the competitor of God's seal found in the seventh-day Sabbath.

For Mrs. White the third angel predicted the time when all men will have to face the basic questions about the authority and justice of God's law. In the final struggle every living person will have to reveal his basic loyalty by the day he chooses to worship on. Revelation 14:12, she pointed out, calls everyone to keep the "commandments of God, and the faith of Jesus." Only by this faith and this obedience will men escape the doom threatened in the third angel's message.

Shortly before the coming of Christ, when everyone has decided between the seal of God and the mark of the beast, probation will close for all men—none will ever be able to change sides again. Mrs. White quoted Revelation 22:11, 12 as the decree Christ will issue at that time, and compared it to the closing of the door of the ark a few days before the Flood. Then will come the great time of trouble, with the righteous standing under a death threat from the wicked and the latter suffering the seven last plagues.

Although threatened with boycott and death, the true people of God will be secure under the protection of angels from heaven. At the time of their greatest extremity Christ will arise to vindicate His own honor and deliver His people. Appearing in the clouds of heaven, He will raise the righteous dead, change the righteous living to immortality, and take them all to heaven. The living wicked will perish from the brightness of His appearing, and Satan will be imprisoned on the desolate earth during the millennium. The saints in heaven will sit in judgment on the wicked, and after the thousand years God will release Satan from his imprisonment by the resurrection of the evil dead.

Then Christ will descend to earth with His saints and the Holy City. After organizing to attack, the wicked will find themselves stopped by the judgment of the great white throne. A panoramic replay of human history will convict them of their sins and lead them to confess that Jesus is Lord indeed. Then the fires of God will pour out to cleanse the earth.

After the fire has done its work, Christ will re-create the earth as the home of His people. The only reminder of sin will be the marks of the Crucifixion. Ellen White's final word was that all things will finally declare that God is love.

The Three Angels' Messages as the Basis of Ellen White's Eschatology

Her description of final events has every major theme noted in the three angels' messages of Revelation 14:6-12 in the context of chapters 12 and 13. The investigative judgment in heaven that goes on while the believers are calling men to worship God on earth fulfills the first angel's message. The conflict between the seal of God and the mark of the beast comes as a result of the third angel's message. The seven last plagues are part of the wrath threatened in the same message, and Revelation 13:11-17 predicts the persecution of the righteous. The difference between her and the Millerites was that the Millerites viewed Christ as coming after the second angel's message, while she saw Him returning after the third.

ELLEN HARMON IN THE MILLERITE MOVEMENT

Ellen White's theodicy originated in these scriptural messages. They reveal the themes of conflict over God's law and of loyalty to Him. There has to come a time when the Lord will convince all men of their sin and His righteousness. Righteous and wicked alike must recognize His justice and mercy. The righteous have their questions answered during the millennium, while the panoramic review before the throne convicts the wicked.

The three angels' messages reveal what Jesus has been doing in heaven since 1844 and what His church should be accomplishing on earth. Establishing the events and issues of the last days, they lay on the people of God the need for personal reformation and public proclamation to prepare for the return of Christ. They explain why Jesus did not come in 1844, and at the same time affirm that He will return soon. So important are these messages to our understanding of Mrs. White's eschatology that we must study her convictions in some detail.

She consistently held that the 1844 experience had made the church's pioneers into Seventh-day Adventists. The three angels' messages had as their purpose to prepare a people to meet God. She made them a key to interpreting other parts of the Bible. Those who had not passed through the Millerite experience, she wrote, faced a real danger of arriving at erroneous views in their study of the Scriptures. As a result she urged them to believe on "their word" (that is, on the testimony of those who had been a part of the 1844 events).[10] The doctrines they had developed were "testing truths" essential for salvation. To reject such an application of the three angels would destroy the very foundation of their faith. Consequently, she pronounced a woe on anyone who would move a "pin or peg" in those messages.[11]

Ellen White was certain that the very essence of the Seventh-day Adventist Church would change if it altered its understanding of the three angels. "The subject of the sanctuary was the key which unlocked the mystery of the disappointment of 1844. It opened to view a complete system of truth, connected and harmonious, showing that God's hand had directed the great Advent movement, and revealing present duty as it brought to light the position and work of His people."[12] The three angels of Revelation 14:6-12, therefore, supplied the meaning for their lives.[13] They gave the church its unique mission: "In a special sense Seventh-day Adventists have been set in the world as watchmen and lightbearers. To them has been entrusted the last warning for a perishing world."[14]

In 1850 White urged that while the Bible continued many truths, what the believers needed at that time were such subjects as the sanctuary, the 2300 days, the commandments of God, and the faith of Jesus—all being integral parts of the three messages.[15] Eight years later she wrote that the third angel lighted up the past, present, and future.[16] And in 1903 she warned that nothing must disturb the foundation laid in 1842-1844. It was "as the Rock of Ages," her constant guide.[17] The "old truths" given at the beginning the church must still herald far and near.[18]

At the end of her ministry she retained the same conviction: "We have nothing to fear for the future, except as we shall forget the way the Lord has led us, and His teaching in our past history."[19] Thus she raised the early Adventist experience to a place of authority second only to the Bible itself.

How Mrs. White kept her faith in spite of the Disappointment

Because it was so important to her eschatology, Mrs. White went to great lengths to defend the 1844 proclamation in the face of the Great Disappointment. In her first vision she saw the believers traveling to heaven on a path high above the world.[20] Christ stood at their head, and the

ELLEN HARMON IN THE MILLERITE MOVEMENT

Midnight Cry (the October 22 proclamation) was a great light behind them, shining over the whole way. For those who denied that God was leading them, she wrote, the light went out and they "fell off the path down into the dark and wicked world below." She pictured Christ coming for His people, raising the dead, and taking them all to heaven. There she saw Charles Fitch and Levi Stockman, two Millerite preachers who had died a short time before the expected day.

The vision showed that the Midnight Cry was of God, but Christ's coming still awaited them. It also said that only those who kept their faith would go to heaven at Christ's return. Her seeing Fitch and Stockman in heaven emphasized that those who died in the Advent faith Christ would raise at His second advent. God had not forsaken His disappointed people—Christ was still leading them and would soon come for them.

She took pains to defend William Miller's character against the criticism that he was dishonest or fanatical. He was upright, honest-hearted, she stated, and "possessed an irreproachable moral character and an enviable reputation." He had "more than ordinary intellectual strength," and "sincerely desired to know the truth." Mrs. White defended the idea that truth could come through a self-taught layman by pointing to the fact that God revealed the news of Christ's first advent to shepherds rather than to priests and rabbis. Referring to Miller's "sound principles of interpretation," she argued that "to deny that the days ended at that time was to . . . renounce positions which had been established by unmistakable fulfillments of prophecy." She believed that his reticence to publish his views showed that he did not work from motives of self-aggrandizement. Finally, she pointed to the nearly complete absence of fanaticism in the Midnight Cry movement as another evidence of God's leading.[21]

The question remains, however, as to what really

HOW LONG, O LORD?

enabled her to retain her understanding of Daniel's prophecies when nothing happened on October 22. Widespread confusion followed the Disappointment. Most of Miller's followers gave up their faith in the 1844 date, and some even lost their belief in God. How did Ellen White keep hers?

Two answers surface. The first is the fact that no one, not even his opponents, had been able to refute Miller's computations. The other was the revival she had seen in the movement. She wrote:

> The fruits of the advent movement, the spirit of humility and heart searching, of renouncing of the world and reformation of life, which had attended the work, testified that it was of God. They dared not deny that the power of the Holy Spirit had witnessed to the preaching of the second advent, and they could detect no error in their reckoning of the prophetic periods. The ablest of their opponents had not succeeded in overthrowing their system of prophetic interpretation.[22]

Thus she felt certain that if they renounced their faith and denied "the power of the Holy Spirit which had attended the message," they "would be drawing back toward perdition."[23] She also wrote, "The special blessing of the Lord, both in the conversion of sinners and the revival of spiritual life among Christians, had testified that the message was of Heaven."[24]

> It bore the characteristics that mark the work of God in every age. There was little ecstatic joy, but rather deep searching of heart, confession of sin, and forsaking of the world. A preparation to meet the Lord was the burden of agonizing spirits. There was persevering prayer and unreserved consecration to God.[25]

She was consistent in her attitude throughout her ministry. In 1858 she stated that in the Millerite revival sinners repented and made restitution for their sins. The

ELLEN HARMON IN THE MILLERITE MOVEMENT

Spirit led their affections away from worldly things to a consecration never before experienced. They sought the Lord with fasting and almost constant prayer. Thus they reflected the image of Jesus, for they had made a full consecration.[26]

In 1876 she wrote that their faith in the near coming of Christ had aroused them to seek new strength and grace from God. It had inspired hope, peace, joy, and love for Jesus, the prayer meeting, the Bible, and prayer.[27] Twenty years later she observed that even the search for answers after the Disappointment had been blessed with evidences of the Lord's presence. As the pioneers studied Scripture, "the truth was opened point by point, and entwined with their most hallowed recollections and sympathies."[28] In 1904 she described how they took care during the time of expectation to have every sin confessed when they went to bed at night.[29]

The spiritual attitudes seen during that revival became a model for many of her exhortations. They provided a point of comparison for the greater power that will attend the final proclamation of the gospel just before the end.[30] She wrote: "Would that there were still with the professed people of God the same spirit of heart searching, the same earnest, determined faith."[31] "We should be putting forth even greater effort than was put forth by those who proclaimed the first angel's message so faithfully." They did diligent house-to-house visitation at that time, and "untiring efforts were made to warn the people of the things that are spoken of in God's Word."[32]

It is clear that it was Ellen White's personal experience that enabled her to go on believing while she waited for the explanation that came from Hiram Edson, Apollos Hale, Joseph Turner, and Joseph Bates. Her eschatology, therefore, had its basis in Scripture and its confirmation in the spiritual fruits of Miller's proclamation. Accepting the accuracy of his date, she retained her faith after the

HOW LONG, O LORD?

Disappointment because of the revival she had seen.[33]

Summary and Reflections

William Miller's proclamation inspired Ellen Harmon's faith in the soon coming of Christ and provided the framework for her prophetic interpretations. She differed from him, however, in accepting the heavenly sanctuary explanation of the Disappointment from Hiram Edson, Apollos Hale, and Joseph Turner. This not only affirmed to her God's leading in the Millerite revival but also inspired much of her ministry. Her understanding held that in 1844 Christ began His judgment in heaven. When finished He will return for His people on earth. In the meantime the church must announce His coming and live holy lives to prepare for Him.

Ellen White agreed with other premillennialists in seeing Christ's coming as near while refusing to set dates. She accepted also their historicist approach to the prophecies, with their view of the manner and purpose of Christ's return, and with their concept of the tasks to be done before the end.

She concurred with their rejection of postmillennialism. This teaching, optimistic about the present age, holds that the proclamation of the gospel will eventually succeed in converting most of the world, and thus Christ will come at the end of the millennium to reign over a kingdom already prepared for Him. The premillennialists, on the other hand, are pessimistic about the present age, believing that it will get worse and worse, and that the most they can accomplish is to gather out a remnant who will be ready for Him.

Because of her thoughts about the judgment, Mrs. White wrote a defense of the ways of God similar to those of John Milton and Jonathan Edwards. The cross of Christ provided the great vindication, but the controversy with Satan has to continue so that all men and angels can see

ELLEN HARMON IN THE MILLERITE MOVEMENT

clearly the righteousness of God and the evil of sin.

Here is where most Adventists begin their study of the delayed advent of Christ. They see it in terms of issues that we have to settle and questions that we have to answer. This type of concept leads to the view that Adventists can hasten or delay His coming by their living and preaching.

It was not the great controversy theme but the Millerite revival, however, that came first in Ellen White's eschatology. She had her first vision on the great controversy in 1858, 14 years after the Great Disappointment. For this reason I emphasize the Millerite revival rather than the great controversy theme. While it is not the usual approach, it is the way she actually came to it herself. While we must give her later thoughts on the great controversy their proper place, we must also consider her earlier revelations on the three angels' messages. Only by studying everything in its place can we accurately plot the trajectory of her thought and achieve a balanced answer today.

It was the 1844 experience, summarized in the three angels' messages of Revelation 14:6-12, that provided the basis for her sequence of final events. In addition to predicting the future crisis, however, the same passages set forth the church's duty. The message that all premillennialists proclaimed to the world thus received a last-day application that is the unique responsibility of the Seventh-day Adventist Church. It is this distinctive conviction of the mission of the church, as well as her view of the two phases of the judgment, that distinguishes her ideas from those of other premillennialists.

Mrs. White's convictions about the 1844 expectation were verified in two ways: one was the cogency of William Miller's biblical arguments, and the other was the spiritual power of the Millerite revival, which became a model for all her exhortations. The 1844 experience provided the

HOW LONG, O LORD?

inspiration and framework for her entire eschatology. The three angels explained the past, gave the Seventh-day Adventist Church its commission, pointed to its future, and marked out its unique place among the churches of the last days.

FOOTNOTES

[1] *Spiritual Gifts*, vol. 2, pp. 20-25.
[2] See Joseph Battistone, *The Great Controversy Theme in E. G. White Writings* (Berrien Springs, Mich.: Andrews University Press, 1978).
[3] *The Desire of Ages*, pp. 762, 763. Ellen White's doctrine of the atonement resembles that of Hugo Grotius (1583-1645), who believed that Christ died to uphold the government of God while making it possible for Him to remit sin. Jesus' death served to maintain respect for the law of God.
[4] *Ibid.*, p. 762.
[5] *The Great Controversy*, p. 356.
[6] Major statements appear in *Testimonies*, vol. 6, pp. 10, 14, 15, 31, 453; vol. 9, pp. 11-20, 89-97; *Prophets and Kings*, pp. 185, 275, 299, 624, 650, 651, 717; *The Desire of Ages*, p. 633; *The Ministry of Healing*, pp. 142, 143; and *The Great Controversy*, p. 408.
[7] *Selected Messages*, book 2, p. 108.
[8] The New Testament concept that the last days began with the first advent of Christ does not appear in Mrs. White's writings. She applied such verses as Hebrews 1:1, 2 ("In these last days he has spoken to us by a Son" [RSV]); Romans 13:12 ("The night is far gone, the day is at hand" [RSV]); Revelation 1:3 ("Blessed is he who reads . . . for the time is near" [RSV]); and Revelation 22:20 ("Surely I am coming soon" [RSV]) to modern times. See *The Desire of Ages*, p. 198, for a brief allusion to Hebrews 1:1, 2; *Selected Messages*, book 1, p. 67, for Romans 13:12; *Testimonies to Ministers*, pp. 113-118, and *The Acts of the Apostles*, pp. 583-585, for Revelation 1:3.

The same statement applies to other Bible believers of her time. Nathaniel West, compiler, *Second Coming of Christ; Pre-Millennial Essays of the Prophetic Conference, Held in the Church of the Holy Trinity, New York City* (New York: Fleming H. Revell, 1879), reproduces the papers read at a prophetic conference held in 1878. Their views resembled those of Mrs. White.
[9] *The Great Controversy*, p. 603.
[10] See *Selected Messages*, book 2, pp. 101-117, especially p. 111.
[11] *Ibid.*, p. 104, and *Counsels to Writers and Editors*, p. 26.
[12] *The Great Controversy*, p. 423.
[13] *Early Writings*, pp. 254-258.
[14] *Testimonies*, vol. 9, p. 19.
[15] *Early Writings*, p. 63.
[16] *Spiritual Gifts*, vol. 1, pp. 163, 164.
[17] "Our Duty to Leave Battle Creek," *Review and Herald*, April 14, 1903, p. 19.
[18] "A Worldwide Message," *Review and Herald*, Aug. 20, 1903, p. 8.
[19] *Life Sketches*, p. 196.
[20] *Early Writings*, pp. 13-20.

ELLEN HARMON IN THE MILLERITE MOVEMENT

[21] *The Great Controversy,* pp. 312-314, 317, 328-331, 351, 396-401, 410, 411.
[22] *Ibid.,* p. 405.
[23] *Ibid.,* p. 408.
[24] *Ibid.,* p. 391.
[25] *Ibid.,* pp. 400, 401.
[26] *Spiritual Gifts,* vol. 1, pp. 133, 134, 142, 143, 157.
[27] "Mrs. Ellen G. White, Her Life, Christian Experience, and Labors," *Signs of the Times,* Mar. 3, 1876, p. 100.
[28] "Three Angels and the Other Angel," Manuscript 32, 1896; see also *Selected Messages,* book 2, p. 109.
[29] "The Day of the Lord Is Near, and Hasteth Greatly," *Review and Herald,* Nov. 24, 1904, p. 17.
[30] *Spiritual Gifts,* vol. 1, p. 196, and *Early Writings,* pp. 277-281.
[31] *The Great Controversy,* p. 373.
[32] "Courage in the Lord," *General Conference Bulletin,* May 27, 1913, pp. 164, 165.
[33] Her statement agrees with one made by Dr. Paul Schwarzenau: "Prior to and underlying every particular church doctrine, however objectively it may be based on biblical exegesis and theological argument, are experiences of faith which have left an indelible mark on that doctrine and are the source which consciously or unconsciously determines the questions, inquiries, and teachings of the church in question. . . . The living resonance of the Protestant 'Scripture principle' rests on the fact that Luther had earlier experienced in the depths of despair the converting power of the gospel. . . . And it is very much to the point that Adventist doctrine is rooted in and derives strength from an event which Adventists later referred to as 'the great disappointment'"(*Ecumenical Review,* April 1972, pp. 201, 202).

Schwarzenau's statement points up the fact that experience usually precedes theology. It was true of the 12 disciples. As they associated with Christ they came to see Messianic significance in Old Testament prophecies that no one had recognized as Messianic before. Until Christ actually died and rose again, none of His followers, with the possible exception of John the Baptist (John 1:29) understood that the sacrifices pointed to a dying Redeemer. Their experience with Christ provided the key that unlocked the Old Testament mysteries.

It was true also of Paul, whose theology grew out of his Damascus road encounter. In Romans 6 he reflected on the meaning of baptism, which his readers had already experienced. Romans 6:1-10 is descriptive, not prescriptive.

The same thing happened in the development of the doctrines of the Trinity and the nature of Christ in the early Christian church. Their reflection on their experience with Christ and the Spirit determined their questions about Christ's nature.

CHAPTER III

The Nearness of Christ's Coming

Two streams of thought flow through Ellen White's writings on the time of Christ's return. One sets forth nearness and the other delay. Logically the two contradict each other, but in her books they seem to harmonize well, often appearing on the same page. The task before us is to discover the principles that explain the harmony. First we shall separate the two, looking at nearness in this chapter and delay in the next, and then bring them together in the fifth.

The Sovereignty of God

According to Mrs. White, we can be sure Jesus will return because God is sovereign. She based her confidence in the Second Advent on the Bible as a whole and the time prophecies in particular. Pointing to Christ's birth in Bethlehem, she wrote, "Like the stars in the vast circuit of their appointed path, God's purposes know no haste and no delay." Just as Israel had left Egypt at the end of the predicted 400 years, "so in heaven's council the hour for the coming of Christ had been determined. When the great clock of time pointed to that hour, Jesus was born in Bethlehem."[1] From Galatians 4:4 she inferred that the time of His birth had been predetermined: "When the fullness of the time was come, God sent forth his Son." Behind that verse lay the 70 weeks of Daniel 9:24-27, the same

THE NEARNESS OF CHRIST'S COMING

prophecy that formed the key element in William Miller's predictions.

Writing about Ezekiel's vision of God's glory, she commented that the symbols of the vision revealed a power above that of earthly rulers. The hand beneath the wings of the cherubim told Ezekiel that human events are under divine control. God's purposes have been working out through the movements of the nations.[2]

God is also sovereign in the church. In spite of its checkered history, she said that "not one cloud has fallen upon the church that God has not prepared for. . . . All has taken place as He has predicted through His prophets." Here also her thinking rested on the prophecies. The "cloud" she referred to was the disappointment of 1844, predicted in Revelation 10.[3] The church would be successful in its mission to the world, for "the cause of present truth . . . is destined to triumph gloriously."[4] She said that the church would reach "a signal and triumphant fulfillment" in the last generation, when the warning message would go to all the world and "take out of them a people for His name."[5] In spite of the time of trouble that lay ahead for the church—"her most severe conflict," her "darkest hour"—God would still be sovereign. Mrs. White had no doubt that He would protect His own and give them final deliverance and victory.[6]

Adventists discouraged at the state of the church can gather encouragement from her optimism:

> It is divine power that gives success. Those whom God employs as His messengers are not to feel that His work is dependent on them. Finite beings are not left to carry this burden of responsibility. He who slumbers not, who is continually at work for the accomplishment of His designs, will carry forward His work.[7]

Again she reminded us, "He made full provision for the prosecution of the work, and took upon Himself the responsibility for its success. So long as they obeyed His word, and worked in connection with Him, they could not fail."[8]

Success will come to the church through a special measure of the Holy Spirit. The angel of Revelation 18:1-4 will unite with the angels of Revelation 14 to bring a "loud cry" to the world, just as the Midnight Cry was joined to the second angel in 1844 (again we see her constant orientation to the 1844 movement). The final revival will be greater than that of 1840-1844 or the sixteenth-century Reformation. The latter rain will be more powerful than the early rain of Pentecost.[9] Thus the finishing of the work of the three angels is very much under God's control.

Some evidence suggests that Ellen White considered the time of Christ's coming as fixed. In her first vision she heard the day and hour of Jesus' coming, showing that God certainly knew when it would be.[10] When someone asked her about this later, she wrote, "The apparent tarrying is not so in reality, for at the *appointed time* our Lord will come."[11] She could not tell the date, however, for she said that after the vision she had no remembrance of it.

Even in statements in which Mrs. White implies delay in the second advent of Christ, she includes ideas that point to a predetermined time. One of her earliest references to delay appeared in 1868, in comments on the parable of the master returning from the wedding feast. She wrote then that the "Lord intimates a delay before the morning finally dawns," but then added, "now the moments are fewer than before the passing of the first watch," and "every passing day leaves us one less to proclaim the message of warning to the world."[12]

When she speaks of each passing day as one less to do God's work, she seems to think of a fixed schedule marching toward its climax. She does not picture a moving horizon that always beckons yet never comes nearer, but rather an event whose time is determined by God but unknown by men.

The Time Prophecies and the *Signs of the Times*

It is a surprising fact that while the time prophecies were primary to Ellen White, she treated the signs of the times as secondary. The first 40 years of her public life she wrote little about last-day signs. During the first few years of the existence of the *Signs of the Times,* founded by James White in 1874, her articles dealt with practical godliness, not with events predicting the return of Christ. We find no exposition of Matthew 24 in *Spiritual Gifts* (1858-1864), nor in the *Spirit of Prophecy* volumes (1870-1884).

When she did take up the signs of Matthew 24, she tied them to the prophetic time periods of Daniel 7 and 8. The Lisbon earthquake of November 1, 1755, occurred after the centuries of persecution. The dark day of May 19, 1780, fell within the 1260-year period of papal supremacy but after the persecution had ended. The falling of the stars on November 13, 1833, happened two years after William Miller started his public proclamation.[13]

In her *Desire of Ages* exposition 54 years after 1844, she presented the same succession of events. First she described the destruction of Jerusalem, then the centuries of apostasy and persecution, finally the signs in the heavens.[14] In 1881 she wrote that the signs of the times proclaimed the end of all things at hand, but immediately added, "Prophecies fulfilled have become facts of history, clearly defining our position."[15] It is the fulfilled prophecies that define our position, not the signs. The prophecies point to the great landmarks, which show we are almost home.[16]

In *The Desire of Ages* Ellen White mentions Matthew 24:34 for the only time in her writings. She wrote:

> He says of those who see these signs, "This generation shall not pass, till all these things be fulfilled." These signs

HOW LONG, O LORD?

have appeared. Now we know of a surety that the Lord's coming is at hand.[17]

If she had believed that "generation" could be used to set a date for the Second Coming, she surely would have mentioned it at that time, 65 years after the meteoric shower of November 13, 1833.[18] On the contrary, she ruled out all date-setting by referring immediately to Matthew 24:36: "The day and the hour of His coming Christ has not revealed."

The most she would say about verse 34 was that the Second Advent is "near," and therefore demands constant readiness on our part. Her refusal to use it to set a date results not only from verse 36, but also from her foundation in the time prophecies. Since they are past, Jesus is coming soon; but for the same reason no one can set a date: they are *past*, and she did not see another application for them in the future.

The only specific events in her lifetime that Ellen White mentioned as signs were earthquakes and Sunday laws. She pointed to the 1906 earthquake in San Francisco[19] and the 1909 earthquakes in Italy and Sicily.[20] Outside of *The Desire of Ages* and *The Great Controversy* expositions of Matthew 24, she made no further reference to the Lisbon earthquake, the celestial signs of 1780 and 1833, the fall of Turkey, or the other evidences mentioned by the Millerites.[21]

Mrs. White pointed to the agitation for Sunday laws in the mid-1880s as an indication that the final crisis was at hand.[22] The authorities convicted Adventists for working on Sunday in several of the Southern states and Canada.[23] In 1888 Senator H. W. Blair, of New Hampshire, introduced a bill in Congress that tried to make Sunday the holy day for the nation.[24] During Mrs. White's sojourn in Australia (1891-1900), similar efforts there attempted to enforce Sunday sacredness and have God acknowledged in the Constitution.[25]

THE NEARNESS OF CHRIST'S COMING

In such events she saw the beginning of the final crisis. God keeps an account of the sins of the nations, and the efforts to enforce Sunday observance added to the total. The "rapidly swelling figures" showed that the time for God's visitations had nearly come.[26] The time of trouble was just before the church. Prophecies were being fulfilled, old controversies were reviving, and new ones were springing up. "If any delay," she warned, "the character of God and His throne will be compromised."[27]

When she wrote about the signs of the times, Mrs. White referred more often to general conditions than to specific events. Increasing wickedness was a common sign of the end, along with violence, contempt for the law of God, corrupt courts, intemperance, oppression, and constructing giant buildings with money gained through oppression of the poor. Wickedness would prevail as in the days of Noah. All of it proclaimed in thundering tones that the hour of God's judgment was come and the end of all things was at hand.[28]

When Ellen White referred to calamities in general, it was always to make a moral appeal. If men would not heed God's voice through the Spirit, then He would speak through judgments, calling the solemn warning, "Be ye also ready." They forced them to make the great decisions.[29]

At the beginning of the twentieth century Mrs. White wrote several times of preparations for international conflict. God was restraining the forces of war while His servants were being sealed, yet at the same time prophecies were being fulfilled.[30] Her moral appeal based on such preparations was that believers had no time to spend in faultfinding and contention, no time to lose in doing the work of God and in getting ready for the great day.[31]

Sometimes she mentioned signs of the times without pointing to any specific examples at all.[32] The particular signs are not important. What is vital is the fact that we are living in the age of signs—the signs are always the basis of exhortations. Because of them Christians must now show practical godliness in their daily lives, awake out of sleep and accept Christ's gift of righteousness, study their Bibles, and live soberly in the world. They are to keep their sins always confessed, purify themselves, show true godliness, transfer their treasure to heaven, and thus reflect the light of God as His representatives.[33]

Besides living holy lives, believers must also preach the gospel, must give the last message of mercy and warning to the world. They must "work, O work! keeping eternity in view." Believers are soldiers doing their duty, that the world might hear the warning.[34] Because the task must be done in a short time, the workers must be trained speedily.[35] The signs exert a constant pressure toward holy living and zealous witnessing.

There is a certain ambiguity about the signs in Mrs. White's writings. She says on one hand that they proclaim in thundering tones that the hour of God's judgment has come, but on the other that the day of God approaches with "footsteps . . . so muffled that it does not arouse the world from the deathlike slumber into which it has fallen."[36] The signs speak in thunder tones to believers but in muffled footsteps to unbelievers. That is why she calls us to awake, watch, and pray.

Since many of the signs are ordinary historical events that every generation could see in its own time, we could ask why she believed they were more urgent in her time. The answer is her orientation to the 1844 movement. At that time conditions that have characterized every age took on special significance. After 1844 all wickedness and all calamities became signs of the end. It is irrelevant to ask whether wickedness is increasing. The point is that after 1844 it is a sign of the end as it has not been before. Ellen White knew she was living in the age of signs.

THE NEARNESS OF CHRIST'S COMING

The Time Known

During most of her life Ellen White expected to live until Christ returned, a point she indicated in at least six statements written between 1849 and 1888. In 1849 she held that the period for Jesus to be in the Most Holy Place was nearly finished and time could last but a very little longer.[37] She identified herself with those who would live at the commencement of the time of trouble and go out to proclaim "the Sabbath more fully."[38] A year later she said that "time is almost finished, and what we have been years learning, they [newcomers to the faith] will have to learn in a few months."[39]

Six years later she stated that people attending a conference in Battle Creek would "remain upon the earth, to be translated at the coming of Jesus."[40] We must, however, take the statement in context: "I was shown the company present at the conference. Said the angel: 'Some food for worms, some subjects of the seven last plagues, some will be alive and remain upon the earth, to be translated at the coming of Jesus.'"

The main point here was not the time of Christ's coming but pride of dress. Why, she argued, should believers spend time and money decorating "their poor, mortal bodies?" Some wasted hours "studying this or that fashion to decorate the poor, mortal body," which might "in a few days be food for worms." "The very ones that profess to be washed by the blood of Jesus, spilled for them, can dress up and decorate their poor, mortal bodies, and dare profess to be followers of the holy, self-denying, humble Pattern." In view of the context, then, it is not right to emphasize her supporting statement that some would live until the end.

Just before the Civil War she commented about the last call of the third angel going "even to the poor slaves, and the pious among them poured forth their songs of rapturous joy at the prospect of their happy deliverance. Their masters could not check them; fear and astonishment kept them silent."[41] In 1883 she wrote of some aged workers that "they may be permitted to remain till Christ shall be revealed in the clouds of heaven," or "they may drop out of the ranks at any time, and sleep in Jesus."[42]

Five years later she declared that some who were then alive would see the prediction verified and hear the voice of the archangel.[43] Three times in her article she referred to the *time* prophecies upon which she based her confidence. The purpose of the doctrine of the near advent of Christ, she held, was to make men fear the Lord. It was not enough to believe that He would come sometime in the future—it must be soon. Everyone must constantly live with reference to that day.

The following year (1889) she again identified herself with the final generation: "We are living in the last days, and the generation that is to witness the final destruction has not been left without warning of the hastening judgments of God."[44]

While we find no later such definite statements that she expected to live until the end, she continued to write that Christ would truly come soon. Even when the drive for Sunday laws faded after 1895, she continued to remind her readers that the "great crisis," the *stupendous crisis* in the history of the world, was just ahead.[45]

Because Mrs. White believed in the soon coming of Christ, she seldom used the risk of sudden death as a motive in her exhortations.[46] Although she usually spoke of Christ coming "soon," some evidence suggests that in her own mind she had a rough time frame of between one and twenty years: "You will not be able to say that He will come in one, two, or five years, neither are you to put off His coming by stating that it may not be for ten or twenty years."[47] What did Ellen White intend by her statements? How did she regard them herself? She lived long enough to see that they were not fulfilled, yet we find no indica-

THE NEARNESS OF CHRIST'S COMING

tion that she experienced any "crisis of delay."

It would be easy to join her critics who said she was simply wrong. One of them charged her with being a false prophet because she had been talking of the soon return of Christ for nearly 40 years, but He had not come yet.[48] But if we do that, we miss the chance of really understanding her. Because she condemned all date-setting, it cannot be that here she tried to do what she herself disapproved of. It is more likely that her statements simply show her taking the nearness of Christ's second advent seriously.

We must keep one fact in mind as we examine her writings. In each statement on Christ's return the moral appeal is primary and the time element secondary. Her declaration that Jesus had nearly finished His time in the Most Holy Place supported an admonition to take time for Bible study and receive the seal of God.[49] The prediction about preaching the Sabbath more fully at the commencement of the time of trouble was part of her 1847 vision on the importance of the Sabbath.[50] We have already noted that her description of some being food for worms and some living until the end comprised part of an exhortation against pride in dress. The expectation that the last call would go to the poor slaves was a prediction about the power of that last call—"strength far exceeding the midnight cry."[51] The purpose of the 1888 word that some then alive would see the final events was clear from the title of the article "Cast Not Away Your Confidence."[52] In each case she used nearness to motivate holiness.

The fact is that the passing years little affected Mrs. White's faith in the soon coming of Christ. In 1875 she described meeting some aging believers in Maine who had first heard the message from her husband in his early ministry. Now they understood the doctrine more fully and had a more firm and rich experience in it. They spoke of their hope and faith with animated countenance as they looked forward to Christ's coming.[53] Again in 1884, at the

HOW LONG, O LORD?

Syracuse, New York, camp meeting, she met other aged workers whose expressions lit up with fresh assurance as they listened to the presentation of the truth that had kept their hearts warm through the years.[54] It is clear that this faith has a power far greater than that of a mere fixed date, a power undisturbed by the passing decades.

Time Unknown

Although God is sovereign, Mrs. White refused to set dates. The 1844 proclamation had been "ordered of God," but He would not approve any later calculations.[55] In 1851 she declared that time had not been a test since 1844 and never would be again. The third angel's message would be proclaimed, but "it must not be hung on time." It was "stronger than time can be."[56]

Mrs. White applied Matthew 24:36—"No man knows the day or the hour"—to her own time, parting company with the Millerites, who argued that the time had arrived when the day and the hour *could* be known. She took the verse at face value because of her foundation in the three angels' messages. Because the time prophecies had ended, the coming of Christ was near, but no one could establish any further date.

Ellen White did not make a chart of final events to tell how much time remained. Rather, she wanted to prepare a people to meet Christ. Her purpose was evangelistic. She hoped that through her work people might "be delivered from the power of darkness, and become 'partakers of the inheritance of the saints in light.'"[57]

Apparently contradicting this statement is the fact that between 1884 and 1905 she wrote that the investigative judgment was about to pass to the cases of the living.[58] Since the judgment of the righteous dead had been going on almost 40 years, therefore the judgment of the living must be about to begin. Jesus' return could not be long delayed. All during this 21-year period Mrs. White clearly

THE NEARNESS OF CHRIST'S COMING

expected the Lord to come almost immediately. Even here, however, she refused to set a date, for in 1889 she denied a rumor that the judgment had *already* started on the living. She insisted she *knew not* when that would be.[59]

Ellen White saw two dangers in date-setting. On one hand, dates once passed throw "contempt upon all efforts to explain the prophecies," and cast "reproach upon the great Advent movement of 1843 and 1844." On the other, those placed too far off lead people to "rest in a false security."[60] Even a date just six months in the future would militate against the believers' "going to God daily and earnestly desiring to know their present duty."[61]

She originally wrote this on June 21, 1851, rebuking some who expected Christ to come that fall and were selling their property in preparation for it. If they had gone to God to know their duty, they would have kept the property. A sermon, preached at Lansing, Michigan, on September 5, 1891, mentions a warning given to another who was date-setting in 1884. Still another appeared in 1894. The source of inspiration in this case, she dryly noted, was the morphine given him for pain in his terminal illness.[62]

Any such message, Mrs. White said, would be false. *Any* date-setting would push the coming of Christ further off than a "near" expectancy. Even six months was not soon enough. Instead of speculating about times and seasons, she urged believers to yield to the Holy Spirit and give the bread of life to others. Speculations diverted men's minds from present truth and present duty.[63]

Mrs. White said she had no special light as to when probation would close, but it was time to work while the day lasted. Believers were to be ready constantly, as though each day were their last. They must live soberly, diligent to be without spot and blameless, always working for God—sharing the message of the coming of Christ.[64]

In the light of such warnings that no one knows the

day or the hour, it is plain that Mrs. White did not intend that anyone should use her own statements to establish dates. Her foundation in the 1844 prophecies led her to believe that Christ would come soon, but the same prophecies also led her to refuse all new timetables. Thus she steered a middle course between excitement and apathy, either of which would destroy spirituality.

Nearness Impels Holiness

Motivated by her belief in the soon return of Christ, Ellen White carried a profound pastoral concern for holy living. Such a faith should always produce ethical results. We shall now examine the relation between White's belief in the near advent of Christ and her many exhortations. Five reasons call for such a study.

1. The three angels' messages of Revelation 14:6-12 not only proclaim the near return of Christ but also sound a ringing call to repentance and godly living. We cannot separate the two. White once wrote that "every true reform has its place in the work of the third angel's message."[65]

2. Such a study is necessary in order to compare her with other believers in the Advent during her time who also called for holiness.

3. We must note what kinds of activities she called for. Some people today are laying in stocks of food and weapons against the turmoils of the last days. What did she advise us to do?

4. In examining her exhortations, we hope to find clues to how she defined the nearness of Christ's coming, and whether her understanding changed with the passing years.

5. Finally, because most Adventists understand Ellen White to teach that Christ is waiting until a significant number of believers attain a certain level of preparedness, we must see what she herself taught. When we find that

THE NEARNESS OF CHRIST'S COMING

she used both nearness and delay as motivations for the same exhortations, we may achieve a better balance in our attitude toward the delay.

Like the biblical prophets, Mrs. White made numerous calls to holiness, but many of hers had as their explicit motivation the soon coming of Christ. The bright light of the Midnight Cry in her first vision cast its rays over her whole ministry.

Basic to all her admonitions were certain fundamental attitudes. She called her readers to deny self, die to the world, and reflect the image of Jesus.[66] "The perils of the last days are soon to come upon us. . . . We need now the sword of the Lord to cut to the very soul and marrow of fleshly lusts, appetites, and passions."[67] "This is no time for trifling or self-seeking. If the times in which we are living fail to impress our minds seriously, what can reach us?"[68] Self-denial in view of the imminent return of Christ involves "greater humility, greater purity, and greater faith."[69]

Although not her only motivation, the soon coming of Christ was certainly a major factor behind all Mrs. White's exhortations. She wrote, "Live and act wholly in reference to the coming of the Son of man."[70] Because the Advent was near, the believers should talk it, pray it, live it, and make it a part of their lives.[71] To workers in the southern United States she advised that they were to be filled with the spirit of Christ's second advent, so that whether working in the field, building a house, or preaching the Word, they might be ready for Him.[72]

Mrs. White often urged her readers to give in order to support the messengers who proclaimed the three angels' messages.[73] They were to study the Bible, for they did not have time for unimportant reading. One purpose of such study was that they might know "the great landmarks," referring to the time prophecies.[74] Always they should avoid letting business cares overwhelm them so that they had no time to give heed to solemn truths,[75] but they were still to be faithful in the ordinary pursuits of life: faithfulness in the least would show them ready for much.[76]

Early in her ministry White used the near Advent as a motive to warn against "pride of dress and appearance." At the same time she found some who made a virtue of being dirty and unkempt and advised them that in view of Christ's soon return they ought to keep their homes neat and in order.[77] She urged religion in the home, along with individual purity.

Her emphasis on health reform stemmed from her belief in the third angel's message and the need to be fitted for translation. She said health reform was just as closely connected with the third angel's message as the arm and hand are with the body.[78] The reason she called it a part of the third angel's message became clearer when she wrote in connection with temperance reform that "every true reform has its place in the work of the third angel's message."[79] The third angel's message called for holiness, and she saw health reform in general and temperance in particular as contributing to holy living. Good health was good religion.

Ellen White's writings on educational reform also had their basis in her eschatology. She wrote that because the Lord was coming soon to take the faithful to the school in heaven, we in our earthly schools ought to meet a standard "very much higher than do those who do not believe these solemn truths."[80] Education had as its purpose preparing the student "for the joy of service in this world and for the higher joy of wider service in the world to come."[81] Although she looked to heaven she did not neglect earth, for the best way to prepare for the future is to make wise use of the present.

White espoused several other reforms without directly mentioning the coming of Christ. Many were popular in the country at the time. Temperance societies were orga-

THE NEARNESS OF CHRIST'S COMING

nized in the 1820s. Educational reform permeated the air. Dancing, theatergoing, and gambling became suspect along with drinking. And by the middle of the century the churches were beginning to see their duty to the poor.[82]

Actually we can say that eschatology stood behind all her reforms. A theologian would maintain that her apocalyptic expectations were the foundation of her prophetic exhortations. The great purpose of her ministry was to make ready a people to meet the Lord. She took popular reforms of her time and incorporated them into her preparation for the coming of Christ.

Occasionally Mrs. White was quite pessimistic about the readiness of the believers. Several times she wrote that scarcely one in 20 of those on the church books was prepared to close his earthly history.[83]

On the other hand, she expressed optimism in her declining years. To the General Conference in 1913 she wrote, "The cause of present truth, to which we are giving our lives and our all, is destined to triumph gloriously."[84]

Underlying all her exhortations lay the basic call to be loyal to Christ. It was the heart of her understanding of the three angels' messages. Men must "empty the soul temple of every defilement, and let the Spirit of God take full possession of the heart, that the character may be transformed."[85]

Wait, Watch, Work, and Pray

Ellen White often used these four terms to describe the attitudes believers should maintain as they wait for Jesus to come. She applied them literally to the disappointed believers of 1844 by saying they waited and watched for further light on their experience, which meant that they cherished what they had and continued to search the Scriptures for more.[86]

Elsewhere she wrote that the waiting and watching Adventists showed that they were strangers and pilgrims on earth. While others sought to secure earthly treasure and lived as though the time were long, the saints were seeking the better heavenly country.[87]

Waiting could mean praying. Watching could involve witnessing to others. Then again, she connected working with improving one's talents for Christ. Watching might mean taking the proclamation of the near Advent seriously, as Noah and Lot did the warnings of destruction in their time. Thus the watchers purify their souls by obedience to the truth. Those who wait, watch, pray, and work will cultivate heart-holiness. Of those who did not show such attitudes, Mrs. White wrote that idle expectancy led them to deficiency of character. They were following the first great apostate.[88]

She did not use the words *wait* and *watch*, however, in connection with the signs of the times. Rather, she advised her readers to watch for the least unholy promptings of their nature, and watch the work of their adversaries lest they gain an advantage in deceiving souls.[89] They were to watch and pray as though each day were their last, and they were to be sober but not to cherish sadness and gloom.[90]

These four words, therefore, express the general attitudes that believers ought to hold in the last days. Rather than calling us to study the newspaper for last-day events, they tell us how to live. We have more to do than idly wait for Jesus to come. Such commands are a constant call to reform.

Ellen White's Relation to the Holiness Movement

Because of her emphasis on holiness in preparation for Christ's return, we shall consider her relationship to the so-called holiness movement. It was a revival emphasis that, protesting the decline of discipline, arose in Methodism in the last half of the nineteenth century. Leaders who became well known for their preaching and books were A.

THE NEARNESS OF CHRIST'S COMING

T. Pierson (1837-1911), F. B. Meyer (1847-1929), A. J. Gordon (1836-1895), and the South African Andrew Murray (1828-1917). Mrs. White had books by Murray, Meyer, and Gordon in her library when she died.[91] Her emphasis on perfection and holiness resembled theirs.

One of the holiness leaders was Hannah Whitall Smith (1832-1911), author of the classic *The Christian's Secret of a Happy Life* (New York: Fleming H. Revell, 1941 [1875], whose chapter topics are quite close to those of Ellen White's *Steps to Christ*. Still another individual influential in the holiness movement was Phoebe Worrell Palmer (1807-1874), whose Christian experience was similar to that of young Ellen Harmon, although she never claimed to receive visions and dreams from God. At the time of her death Mrs. White had Palmer's books *Faith and Its Effects* and *Entire Devotion to God* in her library. It is obvious that they grew up in similar circles and expressed their experiences in parallel terms.

According to L. E. Froom, correspondence between the Millerite preacher Charles Fitch and the Palmers indicated that they may have learned of the Advent doctrine through him.[92] Fitch wrote the Palmers that he preached on "holiness in the afternoon, and on the Second Advent in the evening." Mrs. Palmer authored the Advent hymn "Watch, Ye Saints," still familiar to Seventh-day Adventists today. In Fitch, the Palmers, and Ellen White, the holiness and the Advent emphases united.

Could we call Mrs. White a holiness prophet?[93] There is much evidence to support such an idea. They share many common ideas, but we must also recognize distinct differences. Let us compare Ellen White with Phoebe Palmer.

Both leaders stressed the need for unconditional surrender of one's body and property to the control of Christ, and said that it must be constant.[94] Each carried a heavy burden for their young friends and expressed it in similar terms.[95] White and Palmer spoke of stars in the crowns of the redeemed in heaven representing individuals they had won on earth.[96] The two women quoted Revelation 22:11, 12 as referring to the close of the human probation on earth, although Mrs. Palmer saw it at the moment of death, while Mrs. White put it just before the coming of Christ.[97] In their youth, each had similar visions of Jesus and His look of love toward them.[98]

Mrs. Palmer and Mrs. White both emphasized that one sin could keep a person out of heaven, although Ellen White called it a "cherished" sin.[99] Both said the human body is a temple for the Holy Spirit, although Palmer limited it to proper dress, while Mrs. White based her entire health reform program on it.[100]

The two leaders agreed that the Christian never gets beyond the assaults of Satan. Mrs. Palmer said that to believe in eternal security in the present life would be "the dreadful doctrine denominated 'perfectionism,'" which Mrs. White called "holy flesh."[101] Both spoke of being willing to die rather than offend God knowingly, although Mrs. Palmer applied it to herself, while Mrs. White applied it to the apostles and prophets.[102]

For all their common expressions, however, important differences did exist between the two women. Mrs. Palmer believed that the altar upon which the Christian is to lay himself and his property is Christ, and since the altar sanctifies the gift placed upon it, the moment the believer makes his surrender as a living sacrifice he is perfectly sanctified and holy, saved from all iniquity.[103] Mrs. White spoke of the altar also, but never of instant sanctification, saying rather it is the work of a lifetime.[104] Furthermore, Mrs. Palmer emphasized the sacrifice that the believer makes for God, while Mrs. White gives more stress to the sacrifice Christ has made for man.[105]

We conclude that Ellen White was indeed a holiness

prophet in the best sense of the word. She certainly shared many of the holiness concerns, but did not identify with the holiness movement completely. She had her own unique emphases as she promoted holy living in preparation for the coming of Christ.

Last-Generation Holiness

When the early Adventists learned that Christ began to cleanse the sanctuary in heaven in 1844, Malachi 3:1-3 seemed to throw added light on their experience. Here the prophet quotes the Lord as saying that He will come suddenly to His temple. The "suddenly" meant that His people had not expected to find Him *there*. Ellen White connected Daniel 8:14 with Malachi 3:1-3. The cleansing of the sanctuary corresponded to the Lord's coming to His temple,[106] and it involved purifying the sons of Levi. While the temple is being cleansed in heaven, therefore, there is a special work of purifying God's people on earth. It will make the church glorious, "not having spot, or wrinkle, or any such thing," ready "to stand in the sight of a holy God without a mediator." And it will be done "through the grace of God and their own diligent effort."[107]

Such statements seem to refer to sinless perfection, even though Ellen White never claimed perfection for herself or anyone else. Of herself she commented during her final illness:

> I do not say that I am perfect, but I am trying to be perfect. I do not expect others to be perfect; and if I could not associate with my brothers and sisters who are not perfect, I do not know what I should do.
>
> I try to treat the matter the best that I can, and am thankful that I have a spirit of uplifting and not a spirit of crushing down. . . . No one is perfect. If one were perfect, he would be prepared for heaven. As long as we are not

> perfect, we have a work to do to get ready to be perfect. We have a mighty Saviour. . . .
>
> I am going to keep my mind as much as ever I can on the prominent things of eternal life. They are not dwelt upon enough. I rejoice that I have that faith that takes hold of the promises of God, that works by love and sanctifies the soul. A sanctified soul will not blunder a great deal. . . . The Lord wants us each to do all we possibly can, and fight the good fight of faith.[108]

The nearest she came to recognizing perfection in others was her reference to the apostles and prophets who "would sacrifice life itself rather than knowingly commit a wrong act," but who still "confessed the sinfulness of their nature."[109] Only once did she say, in an encouraging "Letter to an Aged Sister,"[110] that her high standards had been reached. Occasionally she spoke of persons already dead who were sealed and would come up in the first resurrection, as in a letter of condolence to a man who had lost his wife.[111]

Ellen White always held up spotlessness as the goal for all believers (not only those of the last days), but never claimed to have reached it herself. In this she was like John Wesley, who preached the possibility of complete sanctification but never said he had achieved it.

In the statement quoted above, after admitting that she was not perfect, she said, "We have a mighty Saviour," and "I have that faith that takes hold of the promises of God." Her view of being ready to meet Christ was to hold up perfection as the goal and the promises of God as the assurance. The church ought to be perfect and is called to be perfect, yet it cannot claim that it *is* perfect. Perfection is found only in Christ. Ellen White was consistent in saying,

> So long as Satan reigns, we shall have self to subdue, besetting sins to overcome; so long as life shall last, there will be no stopping place, no point which we can reach and

say, I have fully attained. Sanctification is the result of lifelong obedience.[112]

In view of such facts, what did she mean when she said the last-day cleansing would make the church glorious, "not having spot, or wrinkle, or any such thing," ready "to stand in the sight of a holy God without a mediator"? Let us consider four questions as we examine the concept:

1. *What is the nature of this special purification?*

Ellen White here quotes Ephesians 5:27. The spots are character defects that must be removed before we can receive the seal of God. Sometimes she specified particular sins, such as a church's failure to care for the poor in its midst, too great familiarity between men and women, and gratification of animal passions. Then again, she referred to "cherished" sin, which could "eventually neutralize all the power of the gospel." A cherished sin is one that a person does not confess and does not want to give up.[113]

Spotlessness is the prerequisite for receiving the seal of God, the "passport through the gates of the Holy City." The seal is visible when one observes the seventh-day Sabbath, but it will not be placed on those who merely *claim* to keep the Sabbath, only on those who are like Christ in character. The seal means that one's relation to Christ has become a constant way of life. It is a settling into the truth, both intellectually and spiritually, so they cannot be moved.[114]

On the other hand, Ellen White did not believe that the sealed ones are beyond the possibility of sinning. She rebuked those who say "I am saved" in this sense, for they were in danger of trusting to themselves. Being spotless does not mean that we have "holy flesh." That, she said, is impossible in the present life. But we can have "Christian perfection of soul." The first assumes sinless perfection through what man can do. The second refers to trust "in what God can do for man through Christ."[115]

2. *How do we obtain it?*

Ellen White maintained that man has the power of choice, and when he decides to serve God, the Holy Spirit sets him free from the law of sin and death and gives him power to carry out his choice.[116]

God's part in the process includes both justification and sanctification. Justification means that my sins are forgiven and Christ's righteousness is imputed to me. Christ's sacrifice makes a complete atonement, and "pardon covers all transgression." Sanctification is the process that fits me for heaven. Through the Holy Spirit I advance "from grace to grace, from strength to strength, from character to character." I retain my justification through continual surrender.[117]

My part in being cleansed is to believe God's promises, confess my sins, give myself to God, and will to serve Him. As I believe that I am cleansed, God supplies the fact—Christ binds up my wounds and cleanses me from all impurity.[118] Because I love Him, I go about doing good as He did. My face reveals that I have been with Him, for my heart is filled with joy.[119]

When Mrs. White deals with the way of salvation in such books as *Steps to Christ* and *The Desire of Ages*, she assures me that I am pardoned and declared righteous just as soon as I repent and yield to the Lord.[120] But when she writes on the investigative judgment in *The Great Controversy* she seems to delay my justification until the heavenly court considers my name.[121] She wrote that when Heaven opens the books of record and sees that my sins are pardoned and my character is in harmony with the law of God, *then* my sins will be blotted out and I will be accounted worthy of life. Satan accuses me before God as a transgressor, but Christ claims forgiveness for me as He shows my penitence and faith. Then He clothes me with His own righteousness and presents me to the Father without spot, or wrinkle, or any such thing.[122]

What can we say about the two views? The latter picture seems to keep me in suspense until my name comes up in the judgment, while the first assures me that I am forgiven and accepted immediately, just as soon as I confess my sins and turn to Christ. Did Ellen White intend to say that the investigative judgment puts me in jeopardy? Did she see a chance that I might lose my justification when Heaven examines my record?

We must consider the question carefully, because some Adventists have lost their hope of salvation answering it one way, and others have abandoned their faith in Mrs. White's writings by approaching it in another way.

The solution lies in remembering that Ellen White wrote different books for different purposes. The intent of *The Great Controversy Between Christ and Satan* is clear from its title. In it Mrs. White focuses on great cosmic issues, and the investigative judgment appears in that context. Satan accuses the saints as unworthy of God's mercy, but Christ defends them, saying He has graven them on the palms of His hands. The controversy is not between God and the saints, but between God and Satan.

In *Steps to Christ*, however, Satan does not occupy a prominent place, and the book mentions neither the great controversy nor the investigative judgment. Here Mrs. White describes the simple steps I must take in coming to Christ, and assures me:

> You confess your sins and give yourself to God. You *will* to serve Him. Just as surely as you do this, God will fulfill His word to you. If you believe the promise—believe that you are forgiven and cleansed—God supplies the fact; you are made whole, just as Christ gave the paralytic power to walk when the man believed that he was healed. It *is* so if you believe it. . . . It is the will of God to cleanse us from sin, to make us His children, and to enable us to live a holy life. So we may ask for these blessings, and believe that we

receive them, and thank God that we *have* received them.[123]

One of the promises Mrs. White referred to was Isaiah 44:22: "I have blotted out, as a thick cloud, thy transgressions, and, as a cloud, thy sins."[124] The verse does not speak of a future time for blotting out transgression. It is already done if I have confessed and believed.

Nothing that she says about the judgment must be allowed to take away our present assurance. We must grant her the privilege of explaining herself. When she writes on the way of salvation, she cites the promises of immediate acceptance, but when she discusses the great controversy, she speaks of God at last answering Satan's charges in the investigative judgment. In the latter case she is saying more about cosmic issues than about the time when a person is justified. If we recognize these facts, we can see harmony between *Steps to Christ* and *The Great Controversy*.

The two views appear together in Mrs. White's comments on the vision of Joshua and the angel (Zech. 3:1-7).[125] She gives the vision a triple application: first to the Israelites returning from exile in Babylon, then to every sinner who turns to Christ, and finally to the investigative judgment in heaven. The assurance to the first two is immediate, while to the third it seems to be delayed. Even of this final generation, however, the Lord says, "They have repented, and I have forgiven and accepted them," and "God's faithful, praying ones are, as it were, shut in with Him. They themselves know not how securely they are shielded."[126] It is clear, therefore, that Mrs. White did not intend to destroy our confidence in our salvation with her chapter on the investigative judgment in *The Great Controversy*.[127]

The answer to the question of how last-day Christians become spotless is the same as the way of salvation for previous generations. On God's side, it means justification and sanctification. On man's side, it involves believing God's promises, confessing sin, and choosing to serve Him. The investigative judgment confirms the believer's previous justification against the final accusations of Satan. The judgment now in progress lays a solemn obligation upon everyone to afflict his soul by repentance and obedience. It is the "special work of purification" for the last days.

3. *When does it happen?*

Does it mean that the final generation of believers achieves an experience beyond that of all preceding ones? Here is another question that we must answer carefully, lest we fall into the error of setting forth a different way of salvation for the last generation than for others. Some have said that the righteousness that prepares a man to die is by no means sufficient to prepare him for translation, but Paul told us there is "one Lord, one faith, one baptism." Every person indeed has his own unique experience with the Lord, but only one perfect righteousness entitles him to heaven: the righteousness of Christ imputed to him by faith. The last generation will receive "divine approval" and be "well attested by their faith," just like the saints of all past ages (Hebrews 11:2, 39, RSV).

The special purifying of God's people during the investigative judgment is the same as the work of the three angels, which began in 1844. "This work," Ellen White declared, "is more clearly presented in the messages of Revelation 14."[128] Believers in the last days stand under a solemn obligation to afflict their souls, repent, and put away sin, but this is a responsibility that applies to the entire period of the three angels.

Mrs. White always pleaded with her readers to submit to the refining work of God now, to let the truth elevate them now, and to receive the seal of God now, for time is short and will soon be over.[129] She never supplies facts about the future without revealing her clear moral purpose.

HOW LONG, O LORD?

She believed that among her contemporaries God had a people who were following the Lamb wherever He went.[130] They already had the seal, and all who show themselves loyal to Christ during the final test will also receive it.

This seal has a double meaning in her writings. She applies it on one hand to ordinary Christian experience. It is the "sign of the cross of Calvary in the Lord's adopted sons and daughters . . . They have on the wedding garment, and are obedient and faithful to all God's commands."[131] Once she wrote that the Holy Spirit sealed the early disciples on the day of Pentecost.[132] But she also applied it in a special last-day sense. It includes the Sabbath as the outward sign of inward character.[133]

The difference between the last days and earlier times is the judgment in heaven and the sealing on earth since 1844. The eschatological Sabbath sign will be the final issue in the great controversy between Christ and Satan, and the guarantee of security during the time of trouble. It is the mark of complete loyalty to God. But the way of receiving it is the same as that of salvation in all ages: justification and sanctification on God's side; repentance, surrender, loyalty, and obedience on man's, through the power of Christ. Living in the sealing time lends new urgency to man's constant responsibility to his Creator.

4. *Is Christ delaying His coming until this cleansing is done?*

After describing the special last-day's purification of God's people on earth, Mrs. White observed, "When this work shall have been accomplished, the followers of Christ will be ready for His appearing."[134] She did not say that when it was done the Lord *will* come, but that the saints will then be *ready* for Him to come. She wrote that those who live on earth when Christ ceases His intercession in heaven must be spotless and purified, but she did not claim that the end of the investigative judgment awaits their becoming spotless. She presents a sequence of

THE NEARNESS OF CHRIST'S COMING

events for the last days: the judgment in heaven is simultaneous with the cleansing of the saints on earth, followed by the Lord's appearing in glory to execute judgment on the wicked. But she does not teach that His coming depends on the saints' holiness.[135]

Nearness Impels Proclamation

Watchmen for the World

Ellen White felt that faith in the soon coming of Christ should motivate us not only to live a holy life, but also to proclaim the gospel. She saw Adventists as watchmen for the world. They have a responsibility given to no one else, because they alone understand the three angels' messages in their prophetic setting. "Seventh-day Adventists, above all people, should be patterns of piety, holy in heart and in conversation. . . . They look for the near return of Christ in the clouds of heaven."[136]

She exhorted all believers to speak of their faith to everyone they met, because their time for working for God would soon be past. Each day that passed was one less in which to warn the world. In 1881 she wrote that they had only a little while to urge the warfare.[137] By 1904 she declared that very soon the Lord would arise to shake the earth, therefore His people had no time for trivial things.[138] Five years later, however, there remained much work to be done in the cities to prepare the way for the coming of the Prince of Peace.[139] Repeatedly she said that the end was near, but the church still had a great work to finish: how diligently therefore must the believers do it!

During their first generation Mrs. White said little to Seventh-day Adventists about proclaiming the gospel in foreign fields, but in 1872 she began to call for men and women to go there.[140] Counsel she gave on April 1, 1874, helped persuade the General Conference Committee to send J. N. Andrews (1829-1883) to Switzerland later the same year as the first missionary.[141] In the following years she referred to foreign needs repeatedly, particularly when she went to Europe in 1885. She saw them, more and more clearly, tied always to the nearness of the end. Time was short; there was a world to be warned. Her understanding of the task increased, but her view of the nearness of Christ's return did not change. Rather, it became ever more the motive for earnest proclamation.

Sometimes in her writings we find the idea that the church must preach the gospel *so that* Christ can come, but it is not prominent. We find more often that the end is near and *therefore* the church should spread the warning. Vigilance and fidelity have always been required of Christ's followers, but because of the nearness of the end, she urged double diligence.[142] The church must give the message. If it did not present it in favorable times, the church would have to proclaim it under great difficulty. "We have warnings now which we may give, a work now which we may do, but soon it will be more difficult than we imagine."[143]

In 1885 Mrs. White stated that the church was far behind in the task it needed to accomplish. Although the members knew the end was near and that multitudes around them could not be "saved in transgression," yet they took more interest in their trades, farms, houses, merchandise, dress, and tables than in the men and women whom they would meet in the judgment. She mourned that the people of God were asleep. The soon coming of Christ entailed constant obligations of Christian service.

Institutionalizing

Ellen White early guided the young Adventist Church into building institutions to give standing to the proclamation of its message. First came the publishing house, then the sanitarium, later the college and lower schools, and finally food factories and restaurants. They brought a new context for the conviction that Christ would return soon, because institutions are long-range activities. She however, did not see them as putting the Advent farther away. Quite the contrary. The nearness of His coming was also the motive for such activities. The institutions were essential to help proclaim the three angels' messages:

> The influence of these messages has been deepening and widening, setting in motion the springs of action in thousands of hearts, bringing into existence institutions of learning, publishing houses, and health institutions; all these are the instrumentalities of God to cooperate in the grand work represented by the first, second, and third angels flying in the midst of heaven to warn the inhabitants of the world that Christ is coming again with power and great glory.[144]

Her interest in educational reform came from the same source. Education involves character reform, and for that "the time remaining is but too brief a span."[145] Because time is short, the most necessary education is a knowledge of the Scriptures, which will help the students be loyal to the God of heaven.[146] Extraneous subjects had to be excluded. She pleaded for a speedy education for prospective workers. Many activities might be appropriate if we had a thousand years, but time is limited. There simply is not enough for students to multiply their years in school.[147]

Sincere students today sometimes use her writings to resist spending up to 10 years in postsecondary education in order to prepare for a place in the Lord's work. Putting aside the issue of state requirements for licenses in various professions today, we must ask whether she was calling for mere two-year training programs after academy? Let us look at the time and place of her statement.

She was writing from the new field of New Zealand, which sent young people at considerable expense to Battle

Creek College, with the expectation they would quickly return as denominational workers. Mrs. White herself had sponsored some. But once they were in Michigan, Dr. Kellogg encouraged them to extend their years of training and even go for advanced degrees at Ann Arbor. She was using her belief in the soon coming of Christ for a practical purpose: "Send those young people home! We need them in the mission field."

On the other hand, she did not intend to advocate a watered-down program, for two months later she wrote a balancing letter to O. A. Olsen, president of the General Conference. In it she explained that she did not intend the college's education to be superficial, "as is illustrated by the way in which some portions of the land are worked in Australia. The plow was only put in the depth of a few inches."[148]

If Dr. Kellogg ignored the soon coming of Christ in keeping students in school too long, others misused the doctrine in the opposite direction. They argued that if Christ was returning quickly, there was no need to put their money into institutions, no need to use good material for their churches, and no need to spend money on foreign missions.

> Some may say, "If the Lord is coming soon, what need is there to establish schools, sanitariums, and food factories? What need is there for our young people to learn trades?"[149]

Thus the nearness of Christ's coming became an alibi for their selfishness. She replied that they must obey the gospel commission. How could they be ready while failing to carry out His commands? Her reason for using good material in their buildings was that they would not dare to

> dedicate to God a house made of cheap material, and put together so faultily as to be almost lifted from its foundation when struck by a strong wind. . . . And I would not advise

THE NEARNESS OF CHRIST'S COMING

anyone to put worthless material into a house. It does not pay.[150]

She took a commonsense approach to the business of life and the work of the church, while remembering that it could be cut short at any time.

The gospel commission would remain in effect, she stated, until the Lord should bid them "make no further effort to build meetinghouses and establish schools, sanitariums, and publishing institutions." They were to give and "increase the facilities, that a great work may be done in a short time." The Spirit of Christ's advent must so fill them that when He should come He would find them ready, whether they were working in the field, building a house, or preaching the Word.[151]

Building schools, sanitariums, and food factories took the church away from direct preaching, and yet the nearness of Christ's coming remained the motive. Through the institutions the *warning* message became a *healing* one. "It should lead us to do all we possibly can to bless and benefit humanity."[152]

Only by tracing her thought back to the three angels can we understand her admonitions. One would expect that the nearness of Christ's coming would lead her to omit every activity that did not directly prepare for that day. But her concept of the task included faithfulness in *every* legitimate aspect of life, with special emphasis on those that would aid proclamation.

The activities Ellen White urged upon the church were not the kind that can be "finished" so that the believers can someday say they have completed their work, and now it is time for the Lord to do His. Commenting on Matthew 10:23, she wrote that there will always be places to labor, hearts to receive the message, calls for effort in behalf of the institutions, and opportunities for the canvasser to work "as long as the message of mercy is to be given to the world," "until in heaven is spoken the word, 'It is finished.'"[153]

Ellen White believed that the church must constantly remain engaged in its task until the Lord announces its completion. It will not be ready for His coming if it does not. She always put more emphasis on the work to be done and the life to be lived than on the time of the end. Only God knows when the end will come, but the Christian must always work and live in the belief that it is near.

Although Mrs. White did not always mention the return of Christ in connection with her exhortations, it was never far away. Even if the end were not near, she wrote, Christians ought to live lives of simplicity and self-denial, but the end *is* near: "How much more, then, is it incumbent upon this people to manifest unfailing zeal and consecration!"[154] Enoch, who walked with God for hundreds of years, was a representative of those who live amid the perils and corruptions of the last days.

100-Yard Dash Versus Marathon

We can illustrate Ellen White's ethical stance in view of Christ's coming by comparing it to a race. In the Millerite movement of 1842-1844 she was a sprinter in a 100-yard dash. Ellen put everything she had into the revival, taking the little money she earned and using it all to buy tracts and other religious material. She deeply worried about sanctification until she found peace in Christ. Like Phoebe Palmer, she carried a heavy burden for the salvation of her young friends. Laying every weight aside, she concentrated on the short but all-consuming race.

After the Disappointment the Advent believers found themselves running a marathon rather than a sprint, but Ellen White always tried to maintain the zeal, force, and dedication of the 100-yard dash. She urged her readers to give sacrificially to spread the message, and admonished

THE NEARNESS OF CHRIST'S COMING

them to dedicate themselves to the Lord as though each day were their last. As in 1844, they must love Christ rather than the world. Making sure their sins were confessed before they went to bed every night, they were to live in peace and harmony as they had in 1844. And they were to carry the same burden for the salvation of their neighbors that they had then. In every way they were to continue the drive of the dash throughout the marathon. The nearness of Christ's coming exerted constant pressure toward holiness and witness.

Mrs. White's combination of prophetic and apocalyptic attitudes led her both to affirm and deny the world. The way to be ready for the coming of Christ is to do all the good one can in the present life without succumbing to love of the world. Therefore she founded sanitariums to improve our health, food factories to improve our diet, and schools to educate our children. She wanted every Christian to be a source of blessing, yet she did not believe such efforts could set up the kingdom of God on earth, for the world would grow progressively worse in spite of Christian efforts for improvement. Nevertheless, Christians must continue in obedience to God's command until He announces, "It is enough!" The gospel commission is an open-ended assignment.

When Mrs. White led the church to establish institutions, she was adapting to the marathon. The only institution the Millerites had used was the press. They saw no time for anything else. But schools, sanitariums, food factories now became necessary. Of themselves they did not mean that she thought the Lord's coming had been delayed. It was not their existence but their nonexistence that indicated delay in her mind. But in fact the institutions showed that Adventists now expected to be around for some time. The apocalyptic sect developed into a long-term church. Ellen White kept on preaching the soon coming of Christ while leading Adventism into a balanced stance that could cope with the passing decades.

Last-Day Cleansing of God's People

Since a special work of cleansing takes place among God's people on earth while Christ cleanses the sanctuary in heaven, Mrs. White said there is greater urgency behind Christian duties in the time of the end than before. A conviction that Christ is coming soon has always been a powerful motive for holy living, whether it be in the early church, or among the Montanists, the Puritans, or the Adventists.

Sometimes Ellen White described this urgency as living in a constant time of crisis. She spoke of the crisis impending, shortly to come, or already present.[155] The urgency became particularly true after 1888 when the Sabbath-Sunday issue grew prominent, but it was larger than that issue, for the church needed a general spiritual preparation. It included the church's schools, which could prepare the youth by giving them books that would encourage sincerity of life and lead them to the Bible.[156] Since she penned this statement in 1915 when Sunday laws were no longer an issue, we can see that the crisis was existential as well as eschatological. The time was not far distant when the test would come to every soul.[157] Every Christian faces a test in the time of the end when he must decide whether he will be loyal to Christ or not. Because her expectations were not tied to a date on the calendar, she did not experience a "crisis of delay." The crisis was continually impending and always exerting its pressure to choose for Christ and salvation.

Comparison With Other Premillennialists

Seventh-day Adventists share their faith in the near coming of Christ with many other conservative Christians. Two such prophetic systems are those of the dispensationalists and the Pentecostals.

THE NEARNESS OF CHRIST'S COMING

Dispensationalists divide the history of salvation into seven "dispensations," in which God offers differing covenants and conditions of salvation. The last three are the most important: those of law, from Moses to Christ; grace, from Christ to the Second Advent; and the millennium. They believe that the establishment of the nation of Israel in 1948 was the great sign that the period of grace is nearly over.

The rapture will mark the end of the present dispensation, followed by three and a half years of peace, the appearance of the antichrist, and then three and a half years of terrible trials for the Jews. Most of the book of Revelation, this interpretation believes, will be fulfilled during this seven-year period. Christ will appear in the clouds of heaven at its close, to take His place on a literal throne in Jerusalem, from whence He will rule the nations with a rod of iron during the thousand years.

Ellen White shares with the dispensationalists their confidence that the present age is near its end, but she looks for certain events to occur first. Furthermore, her biblical foundation is quite different from theirs. Dispensationalism rests on the conviction that the church is a purely spiritual body that is not involved in biblical prophecies and whose history is entirely separate from that of the Jews. For the church there are no events that must precede the rapture. Mrs. White's basis, on the other hand, is the three angels' messages of Revelation 14, as applied to the church.

Because of their futurism, dispensationalists find it hard to make ethical applications of their beliefs. The events they expect will all occur after the removal of the church from the earth. Therefore they have no effect on the life of the church now. In the notes of the famous *Scofield Bible* we do not find evangelistic appeals based on the coming of Christ. But in Ellen White the judgment now in session provides a powerful motive for ethical living and witnessing.[158]

In charting the future, the dispensationalist offers bare information. A Christian looking at an Israel-centered future based on Old Testament prophecies can be interested only in an abstract way in what will happen after God removes him from the earth. Ellen White, on the other hand, used her eschatology to appeal to man's moral nature. She depicted the future as the climax of the controversy between Christ and Satan and believed that the church has a crucial part to play in the final drama. Every item in her sequence of events was impending and formed the basis of ethical appeals: the judgment, the shaking time, the loud cry, the latter rain, the time of trouble, and the close of probation. She was not an Adventist futurist; her burden was not to reveal the future, but to prepare for it.

The second eschatology we shall compare with Ellen White's is that of the Pentecostals, twentieth-century heirs of the holiness movement. They believe that their movement is God's latter rain bringing in the last fruits of the harvest just before the coming of Christ.[159] The rain of the Spirit is particularly evident in the charismata of the Spirit, notably tongue-speaking and miracle-working.

Ellen White also believed in a latter rain of the Spirit to ripen earth's harvest, but she saw it as a future experience.[160] To be ready for it (here we see her constant evangelistic appeal), believers must daily yield themselves to God. Unlike the Pentecostals, she pointed not to unusual gifts as evidence that Christ's return was near, but to the time prophecies fulfilled in the past.

Ellen White and New Testament Eschatology

Ellen White did not emphasize the New Testament picture of the last days beginning with the first advent of Christ. Such verses as Acts 2:17, 2 Timothy 3:1-6, Hebrews

THE NEARNESS OF CHRIST'S COMING

1:2, James 5:3, 1 John 2:18, 1 Peter 4:7, and James 5:8 she always applied to her own time and the near future. It is clear that their original readers must have applied them in *their* time. The closest she came to the New Testament concept was to say that the kingdom of heaven has two phases, the kingdom of grace and the kingdom of glory, with the latter beginning at the return of Christ.[161]

The reason Ellen White and the other premillennialists of her time placed the time of the end in the modern era was their understanding of Daniel and Revelation. She viewed the prophecies as coming to pass in *her* time, while the New Testament Christians saw them fulfilled in *their* time, namely, in the events of the life, death, and resurrection of Christ. This is why she gave as much space to the events of 1844 as she did to the life of Christ in her earliest presentation of the great controversy theme.[162]

That is not to say that she minimized the life of Christ. She gave it much more space in her later ministry, expanding her presentation on it from the 54 pages in *Spiritual Gifts*, volume 1, to the 835 pages of *The Desire of Ages*, plus four smaller books.[163] The two advents of Christ were related in her mind as seed sowing is to harvest. Throughout her ministry they formed the focus of her theology.

How Soon Is Soon?

How near, then, is near? How soon is soon? As we study Ellen White's sequence of final events, can we tell how much longer we must wait? The answer is no, not since the Sunday-law issue of the late 1880s. If we did know, we would have a much more exact date than she was ever willing to give while she was alive. When we ask how many years we have to wait until the Lord comes, we are asking the wrong question of her. She did not intend to provide a timetable of final events, and those who draw charts based on her writings are misusing her. Never making any charts herself, she wanted rather to prepare a people to meet Christ whenever He might come. Her eschatology is an evangelistic appeal for the present, not a fortuneteller's forecast for the future. It is nearer than any date can be. In the words of William Miller after the Disappointment, it is "*Today*, TODAY, and TODAY, until He comes."[164]

Thus the doctrines represented by the three angels' messages in Revelation 14:6-12 were the foundation and guiding principles of Ellen White's entire eschatology. They marked out her place in the history of salvation, told her she was living in the last days, and gave the church its mission in the world, but did not set a date for Christ's coming.

Summary

After the Millerite revival and disappointment in 1844, Ellen White's thought moved backward to the cross of Christ, as well as forward to His second coming. Her conviction that the 1260- and 2300-year prophecies of Daniel 7-9 spanned the Christian centuries enabled her to avoid the problem of an eighteen-century delay in Christ's coming. It was the fulfillment of the 70-week prophecy that convinced her that God is sovereign: His purposes know no haste and no delay. Because past predictions have been fulfilled, the future is certain.

Ellen White's view of the future grew out of the same prophecies. The concept of the pre-Advent judgment in 1844 led her to reflect on its purpose, which in turn pointed her to the larger questions of the conflict between Christ and Satan. Here was the root of her theodicy—her defense of the ways of God.

The signs of the times always appear in connection with the time prophecies in her writings. Events take on the quality of signs because they occur in the time of the end. Their purpose, however, is not to give bare predic-

THE NEARNESS OF CHRIST'S COMING

tions of the future, but to summon faith and commitment. Mrs. White does not proclaim a sequence of future events so much as she calls for a new quality of life. She speaks more of *what* the kingdom is than of *when* it will come.

The hope of Christ's return has been a dynamic conviction throughout the history of the Christian church. The fact that He has not come yet has not destroyed faith. The failure of expected details has not changed its essence. Although Ellen White herself lived for seven decades after the Great Disappointment, she continued to write that His coming was imminent.

Paul Althaus, a respected twentieth-century theologian, has wisely said that true "biblical eschatology is always the imminent expectation of the end." All serious and living eschatology sees the signs of the end in its own time, pointing to the present moment. The church, he said, must arm itself not for the final battle, which may be far off, but for the one it is facing now—the one that it must fight as though it were the last.[165]

Mrs. White's "soon" did not mean, however, that we actually know nothing about the time of Christ's coming. She felt that the period after 1844 was borrowed time. The Master could come at any time. Instead of looking for a climax that might be a millennium in the future, she expected Christ to appear literally in her lifetime. The time prophecies showed His coming near, but the fact that they were past indicated the date was unknown.

Her eschatology combines themes from the classical prophets (such as Isaiah, Jeremiah, and the minor prophets) as well as from the apocalyptic prophets (Daniel and John). The former denounced social evil, injustice, and oppression of the poor, as well as idolatry. Daniel shared their concern, as we see in his prayer of confession (Daniel 9) and his admonition to Nebuchadnezzar to break off his sins by practicing righteousness and showing mercy to the poor (Daniel 4:27). John in Revelation, however, is con-

HOW LONG, O LORD?

cerned with the saints' relation to God rather than their relation to other men. The purpose of his book is to urge believers to be faithful in times of persecution.[165]

Ellen White's eschatology unites these themes. The three angels proclaim far more than a simple announcement that the end is near. They include every true reform and provide the foundation for all her exhortations. She spoke with a true "prophetic" voice, in both the classical and apocalyptic senses of the word.

FOOTNOTES

[1] *The Desire of Ages*, p. 32.
[2] "Our Present Duty and the Coming Crisis," *Review and Herald*, Jan. 11, 1887, pp. 17, 18; see also *Prophets and Kings*, pp. 535-537.
[3] Manuscript 32, 1896; see also *Selected Messages*, book 2, p. 108.
[4] "Words of Greeting From Sister White," *Review and Herald*, May 29, 1913, p. 515.
[5] *Christ's Object Lessons*, p. 79.
[6] *Testimonies to Ministers*, p. 20; *Prophets and Kings*, pp. 720, 725, 730-733; *Evangelism*, p. 707.
[7] *Prophets and Kings*, p. 176.
[8] *The Desire of Ages*, p. 822.
[9] *The Great Controversy*, pp. 603-613; *Early Writings*, pp. 277, 278; *Christ's Object Lessons*, p. 121; *The Desire of Ages*, p. 827.
[10] *Early Writings*, p. 15.
[11] Letter 38, 1888. (Italics supplied.) All unpublished manuscripts released by the E. G. White Estate for this book are reproduced in the appendix.
[12] *Testimonies*, vol. 2, pp. 192-194; vol. 5, p. 88.
[13] *The Great Controversy*, pp. 54, 55, 304-308, 333-335.
[14] *The Desire of Ages*, pp. 628-632.
[15] "The Advent Faith," *Review and Herald*, Nov. 29, 1881, p. 337.
[16] "The Christian's Hope," *Signs of the Times*, May 29, 1884, p. 321.
[17] *The Desire of Ages*, p. 632.
[18] Neither do we have any evidence that the Gospel writers used the statement to set a date, although they wrote from 30 to 40 years after Jesus spoke.
[19] "The San Francisco Earthquake," *Review and Herald*, May 24, 1906, p. 8; "Even at the Door," *Review and Herald*, Nov. 22, 1906, pp. 19, 20.
[20] "Go, Preach the Gospel," *Review and Herald*, Nov. 17, 1910, p. 7.
[21] She referred briefly to Turkey in a report of a sermon by Uriah Smith: see *Testimonies*, vol. 4, p. 279. P. T. Magan wrote on Turkey in the *Review and Herald*, Aug. 5, 1909, p. 9, but Mrs. White's article, "A Great Revival Needed," on the same page ignored it.
[22] In *Testimonies*, vol. 5, we find two chapters written in 1885 and two in 1889. See pp. 449-467 and 711-720. A number of articles also appear in the *Review and Herald Extra* of Dec. 11, 1888, which sent Adventists out with petitions

THE NEARNESS OF CHRIST'S COMING

against the Blair amendment; Jan. 1, 1889; Nov. 5, 1889; another *Extra* dated Dec. 24, 1889; Apr. 26, 1892; and Nov. 22, 1892.

[23] The story is told in A. W. Spalding, *Origin and History of Seventh-day Adventists*, (Washington, D.C.: Review and Herald Pub. Assn., 1962), vol. 2, pp. 239-262; and William Addison Blakeley, compiler, *Legislative, Executive, Judicial American State Papers Bearing on Sunday Legislation*, rev. and enl. ed. (Washington, D.C.: Religious Liberty Association, 1911), pp. 653-680, 718-726.

[24] Blakeley, pp. 226-228, 360-363; and Warren L. Johns, *Dateline Sunday, U.S.A.: The Story of Three and a Half Centuries of Sunday-law Battles in America* (Mountain View, Calif.: Pacific Press, 1967), pp. 35-41.

[25] Letter 28, 1897.

[26] "Our Present Duty and the Coming Crisis," *Review and Herald*, Jan. 11, 1887, pp. 17, 18.

[27] Manuscript 27, in *Special Testimonies*, Series A, No. 1, p. 67. The sentences quoted probably came from a stenographer's notes. Mrs. White edited them later for publication to read, "Something great and decisive is soon to take place, else no flesh would be saved. The character of God will not be compromised." See "Prepare to Meet the Lord," *Review and Herald*, Nov. 27, 1900, p. 753.

[28] *The Desire of Ages*, p. 633; *Prophets and Kings*, p. 278. She did not see the fulfillment of Matthew 24:14 as a sign of the end, but as a task to accomplish before the end. We will therefore defer our study of this verse until chapter 5.

[29] *The Desire of Ages*, p. 636; *Testimonies*, vol. 8, pp. 11-17; *Prophets and Kings*, p. 276; "What Manner of Persons Ought Ye to Be?" *Signs of the Times*, Oct. 1, 1894, pp. 739, 740; "The Day of the Lord Is Near, and Hasteth Greatly," *Review and Herald*, Nov. 24, 1904, p. 16, and many others.

[30] *Testimonies* (1900), vol. 6, p. 14; see also "A Message to Our Churches," *Review and Herald*, Jan. 28, 1909, pp. 7, 8 (*Selected Messages*, book 1, pp. 221-225).

[31] "The Day of the Lord Is Near, and Hasteth Greatly," *Review and Herald*, Nov. 24, 1904, p. 16; "The Time of the End," *Review and Herald*, Nov. 23, 1905, pp. 6, 7; *Testimonies*, vol. 9, pp. 16, 48.

[32] *Christ's Object Lessons* (1900), p. 227; *The Acts of the Apostles*, p. 260; *Testimonies*, vol. 7, p. 14; *Testimonies to Ministers*, p. 364.

[33] *The Acts of the Apostles*, p. 262; "The Coming Crisis," *Signs of the Times*, Oct. 9, 1901, p. 643; "What Manner of Persons Ought Ye to Be?" *Signs of the Times*, Oct. 1, 1894, pp. 739, 740; and "The Perils and Privileges of the Last Days," *Review and Herald*, Nov. 22, 1892, p. 722.

In the last-named article above Mrs. White also writes, "The time of test is just upon us, for the loud cry of the third angel has already begun in the revelation of the righteousness of Christ, the sin-pardoning Redeemer. This is the beginning of the light of the angel whose glory shall fill the whole earth." L. E. Froom, in *Movement of Destiny* (Washington, D.C.: Review and Herald Pub. Assn., 1971), pp. 369, 370, said on the basis of this statement that the 1888 session of the General Conference was the turning point in the experience of the Adventist Church—Christ could have come soon after that time.

He may have overstated his point, however. She made only one reference to the second advent of Christ in her published sermons at the 1888 conference: "Now, brethren, we are almost home; we shall soon hear the voice of the Saviour richer than any music, saying, Your warfare is accomplished" ("Advancing in Christian Experience," preached Oct. 20, 1888 (see A. V. Olson, *Through Crisis to Victory, 1888-1901* [Washington, D.C.: Review and Herald Pub. Assn., 1966], p. 268). In this sermon Ellen White did not make the time of Christ's return wait for the response of the church. The statement quoted by Froom appeared four years later. Furthermore, we find other statements both before and after 1888 that made the Second Advent just as near.

HOW LONG, O LORD?

[34] "The Day of the Lord Is Near, and Hasteth Greatly," *Review and Herald*, Nov. 24, 1904, p. 16.

[35] *Fundamentals of Christian Education*, pp. 334, 335. She wrote this testimony from Australia on March 21, 1895, at a time when students sponsored to attend Battle Creek College were being encouraged by teachers there to extend their years of study in America, thus depriving the mission field of service. A month later she wrote a balancing letter to O. A. Olsen, General Conference president, saying she was not asking for a superficial education like the Australian farmers who put their plows only two or three inches in the ground. See her letter of April 22, 1895 (in *Fundamentals of Christian Education*, p. 368).

[36] *Prophets and Kings*, p. 278; *Fundamentals of Christian Education*, p. 335.

[37] "To Those Who Are Receiving the Seal of the Living God," broadside, Jan. 31, 1849 (in *Early Writings*, p. 58).

[38] "To the Remnant Scattered Abroad," *Review and Herald Extra*, July 21, 1851 (in *Early Writings*, p. 33).

[39] June 27, 1850, vision, in *Early Writings*, p. 67.

[40] *Spiritual Gifts*, vol. 4, p. 18; *Testimonies*, vol. 1, pp. 131-136.

[41] *Early Writings*, p. 278.

[42] "Notes of Travel," *Review and Herald*, Nov. 13, 1883, p. 705.

[43] "Cast Not Away Your Confidence," *Review and Herald*, July 31, 1888, pp. 481, 482.

[44] "God Warns Men of His Coming Judgments," *Review and Herald*, Nov. 5, 1889, p. 689.

[45] "Preparation for the Final Crisis," *Testimonies* (1900), vol. 6, p. 404; "The Judgments of God on Our Cities," *Review and Herald*, July 5, 1906, p. 9.

[46] We have found only two such statements: in *Testimonies*, vol. 5, p. 487, and "It Is Not for You to Know the Times and the Seasons," *Review and Herald*, Apr. 5, 1892, p. 209.

[47] See "'It Is Not for You to Know the Times and the Seasons.'" *Review and Herald*, Mar. 22, 1892, pp. 177, 178 (in *Evangelism*, p. 221); also "Walking in the Light," *Review and Herald*, Oct. 25, 1881, p. 257; and Manuscript 32, 1896 (in *Selected Messages*, book 2, pp. 113, 114).

[48] One such critic was A. C. Long, of Marion, Iowa, who published a *Comparison of the Early Writings of Mrs. White With Later Publications*, 2nd ed. (Stanberry, Mo: Church of God Pub. House, 1911). The first edition appeared in 1883. See also former Adventist minister D. M. Canright (1840-1919), who turned against the church and became a bitter enemy of Mrs. White, in his *Life of Mrs. E. G. White, Seventh-day Adventist Prophet; Her False Claims Refuted* (Nashville: B. C. Goodpasture, 1953), pp. 240, 241; and *Seventh-day Adventism Renounced* (Nashville: Gospel Advocate Co., 1961 reprint from fourteenth ed., printed in 1914), pp. 146, 147.

[49] *Early Writings*, p. 58.

[50] Ibid., p. 33.

[51] Ibid., p. 278.

[52] *Review and Herald*, July 31, 1888, pp. 481, 482.

[53] Letter 31, 1875.

[54] "Notes of Travel," *Review and Herald*, Oct. 28, 1884, p. 673.

[55] *The Great Controversy*, p. 457.

[56] *Early Writings*, p. 75.

[57] *The Great Controversy*, p. xii. The origin of the expression "shed light on the pathway" in her first vision is apparent.

[58] "The Christian's Hope," *Signs of the Times*, May 29, 1884, p. 321; *Spiritual Gifts* (1884), vol. 4, p. 315; letter 51, 1886; *The Great Controversy* (1888), p. 490; *Testimonies* (1889), pp. 526, 692; vol. 6, p. 130; "Lessons From the Life of

THE NEARNESS OF CHRIST'S COMING

Solomon—No. 9," *Review and Herald,* Nov. 9, 1905, p. 10.

[59] *Testimonies,* vol. 5, p. 692.

[60] *The Great Controversy,* p. 457.

[61] "It Is Not for You to Know the Times and the Seasons," *Review and Herald,* Mar. 22, 29, Apr. 5, 1892. See *Selected Messages,* book 1, pp. 185-191.

[62] *Selected Messages,* book 2, p. 113.

[63] *Review and Herald,* Mar. 22, 1892, pp. 177, 178. Her balanced attitude is the same as that of the well-known theologian G. C. Berkouwer in *The Return of Christ* (Grand Rapids: Eerdmans, 1972), pp. 84-86. He writes that the believer is not to *reckon* but constantly *reckon with* the coming of Christ. It will be unexpected, but not un-expected.

[64] "Consequences of Adam's Sin a Warning to Men," *Review and Herald,* Oct. 9, 1894, pp. 625, 626; "Walking in the Light," *Review and Herald,* Oct. 25, 1881, pp. 257, 258; *The Desire of Ages,* pp. 632-634; "Looking for That Blessed Hope," *Signs of the Times,* June 24, 1889, pp. 369, 370; "The Blessed Hope," *Review and Herald,* Nov. 13, 1913, pp. 1110, 1111.

[65] *Testimonies,* vol. 6, p. 110.

[66] Such statements occur repeatedly throughout her writings. Note especially "The Church the Light of the World," *Testimonies* (1885), vol. 5, p. 457, which warns against taking more interest in moneymaking, trades, farms, houses, and merchandise than in giving the light of the warning messages to others.

[67] "Importance of Seeking True Knowledge," *Testimonies* (1904), vol. 8, p. 315.

[68] "Words of Greetings From Sister White," *Review and Herald,* May 29, 1913, p. 515.

[69] *Testimonies* (1882), vol. 5, p. 88; vol. 9, p. 203.

[70] *Early Writings,* p. 58.

[71] Letter 66, 1901.

[72] Letter 25, 1902.

[73] *Early Writings,* pp. 48-51, 58, 266, 267; *Testimonies,* vol. 6, p. 442.

[74] "To Those Who Are Receiving the Seal of the Living God," broadside, Jan. 31, 1849 (in *Early Writings,* p. 58); *Testimonies,* vol. 5, pp. 18, 19.

[75] "Notes of Travel—No. 6; Loma Linda and Los Angeles," *Review and Herald,* Sept. 5, 1907, pp. 8, 9.

[76] "Preparation for Christ's Coming," *Testimonies,* vol. 4, p. 309; see also vol. 5, pp. 178-182; *Christ's Object Lessons,* pp. 325-365.

[77] *Early Writings* (1854), p. 120; "To the Church," *Review and Herald,* June 12, 1855, p. 246.

[78] *Testimonies,* vol. 1, pp. 486, 487.

[79] *Testimonies,* vol. 6, p. 110; see also *Prophets and Kings,* p. 678: "In the time of the end every divine institution is to be restored."

[80] Letter 25a, 1890.

[81] *Education,* p. 13.

[82] For the history of such reform movements, see Sydney E. Ahlstrom, *A Religious History of the American People* (New Haven, Conn.: Yale University Press, 1972), pp. 426, 427; Timothy L. Smith, *Revivalism and Social Reform: American Protestantism on the Eve of the Civil War* (New York: Harper and Row, Torchbooks ed., 1965), pp. 163-177; Alice Felt Tyler, *Freedom's Ferment* (New York: Harper and Row, 1944, Torchbooks ed., 1962), pp. 308-350.

[83] *Testimonies,* vol. 1, pp. 496, 504, 510, 632; "Christ's Instruction to His Followers," *Review and Herald,* Apr. 26, 1892, p. 258.

[84] *General Conference Bulletin,* May 19, 1913, p. 34; see also the positive statements in *Prophets and Kings,* pp. 720, 722, 731.

HOW LONG, O LORD?

[85] "Christ's Instruction to His Followers," *Review and Herald*, Apr. 26, 1892, p. 258.

[86] *The Great Controversy*, p. 408.

[87] "Worldliness in the Church," *Testimonies*, vol. 2, p. 194.

[88] "Waiting and Working for Christ," *Review and Herald*, Apr. 12, 1898, p. 229; *Testimonies* (1871), vol. 2, p. 673; *Christ's Object Lessons* (1900), p. 325; *The Desire of Ages*, p. 634; "Lessons From the Christ-Life," *Review and Herald*, Oct. 2, 1900, p. 625. The custom of using the four terms together may have started with the 1878 Prophetic Bible Conference in New York City. See Nathaniel West, comp., *Premillennial Essays*, p. 8. See also "The Perils and Privileges of the Last Days," *Review and Herald*, Nov. 22, 1892, pp. 722, 723.

[89] *Testimonies*, vol. 5, pp. 534, 535; vol. 3, p. 572.

[90] *Ibid.*, vol. 5, pp. 148, 200.

[91] Ron Graybill and Warren H. Johns, "A Bibliography of Ellen G. White's Private and Office Libraries," Ellen G. White Estate Document File 825.

[92] *Prophetic Faith*, vol. 5, pp. 537, 538.

[93] One critic who has done so is Ingemar Linden, *The Last Trump* (Frankfurt am Main, Bern, Las Vegas: Peter Lang, 1978), pp. 253-258.

[94] Phoebe Palmer, *Entire Devotion to God* (Salem, Ohio: Schmul Publishers, Rare Reprint Specialists, 1979 [c. 1850]), pp. 48, 65-76; and Ellen White, *Testimonies*, vol. 4, p. 382; *Early Writings*, p. 66, 67.

[95] Palmer, p. 27; White, *Life Sketches*, pp. 41, 42.

[96] Palmer, p. 40; White, *Early Writings*, p. 61; *Testimonies*, vol. 1, p. 198.

[97] Palmer, p. 48; White, *The Great Controversy*, pp. 490, 491, 613.

[98] Palmer, pp. 48-52; White, *Life Sketches*, p. 35.

[99] Palmer, p. 68; White, *Steps to Christ*, p. 33.

[100] Palmer, p. 73; White, *Testimonies*, vol. 2, p. 70; *Counsels on Health*, p. 83.

[101] Palmer, *Full Salvation; Its Doctrine and Duties*, pp. 148-151; White, *Selected Messages*, pp. 31-36.

[102] Palmer, p. 175; White, *The Acts of the Apostles*, p. 561.

[103] Palmer, *Entire Devotion to God*, pp. 65, 69.

[104] White, *The Acts of the Apostles*, p. 560; *Christ's Object Lessons*, pp. 65, 66; *Selected Messages*, book 1, p. 317.

[105] White, *Patriarchs and Prophets*, pp. 66, 67; *The Desire of Ages*, pp. 565, 660, 756, 757.

[106] *The Great Controversy*, p. 426.

[107] *Ibid.*, p. 425. Ten years later Mrs. White applied Malachi 3:1-3 to Jesus' cleansing the Temple in Jerusalem, which was a type of His work of cleansing human hearts from sin. See *The Desire of Ages*, pp. 34, 161; *Prophets and Kings*, p. 700. There is thus a triple fulfillment of the Malachi passage: the Jerusalem Temple, the heavenly temple, and the temple of the heart.

[108] "The Last 153 Days," *Review and Herald*, July 23, 1970, p. 3, quoting a letter from W. C. White to the editor of the *Pacific Union Recorder*, Apr. 23, 1915.

[109] *The Acts of the Apostles*, p. 561.

[110] Letter 299, 1904.

[111] Letter 10, 1850.

[112] *The Acts of the Apostles*, pp. 560, 561. Perfection must be our aim, for we shall never reach higher than the goal we set ourselves, but we fall into heresy if we claim to have attained it. Morris Venden has wisely observed that it is unprofitable to preach perfection, and demonic to preach imperfection. We should preach Christ's perfection, not ours.

[113] *Testimonies*, vol. 5, pp. 211-216, 592; vol. 6, p. 261; vol. 2, p. 453; *Steps to Christ*, p. 34; *Christ's Object Lessons*, pp. 316, 366.

THE NEARNESS OF CHRIST'S COMING

[114] *The SDA Bible Commentary,* Ellen G. White Comments, vol. 7, pp. 969, 970.

[115] *Christ's Object Lessons,* p. 155; *Selected Messages,* book 2, pp. 32, 33. In the latter passage Mrs. White rebukes fanatics in Indiana who claimed that they had holy flesh and were therefore beyond the reach of sin. The perfection she recognized meant a conscience free from condemnation through forgiven sin, and sanctification through surrender to Christ to be molded in His likeness.

[116] *The Desire of Ages,* p. 466; *Messages to Young People,* p. 105.

[117] See *Christ's Object Lessons,* p. 156, the entire section on "Christ Our Righteousness" in *Selected Messages,* book 1, pp. 350-400.

[118] *Steps to Christ,* pp. 51, 52; see also *The Desire of Ages,* p. 266; *Christ's Object Lessons,* p. 158; *Testimonies to Ministers,* p. 147. These books, which she wrote in the 1890s, add much to what she said about perfection in *The Great Controversy* in 1888.

[119] *Selected Messages,* book 1, p. 398.

[120] *The Desire of Ages,* pp. 266, 267. Commenting on leprosy as a symbol of sin, she said that in some cases of healing Jesus did not grant the blessing immediately, but "in the case of leprosy, no sooner was the appeal made than it was granted." There is no suggestion here that the sinner must wait until the judgment for his sin to be forgiven. See also "Two Worshipers," *Christ's Object Lessons,* pp. 150-163, and "Justified by Faith," *Selected Messages,* book 1, pp. 389-398, which affirm that the Lord grants justification and acceptance just as soon as a sinner believes and repents.

[121] "Facing Life's Record," *The Great Controversy,* pp. 479-491. The chapter "Without a Wedding Garment," *Christ's Object Lessons,* pp. 307-319, also presents justification in the context of the investigative judgment. On the other hand, compare the "Two Worshipers" chapter in the same book cited above.

[122] *The Great Controversy,* pp. 482-484.

[123] *Steps to Christ,* p. 51.

[124] *Ibid.,* p. 53.

[125] *Testimonies,* vol. 5, pp. 467-476, and *Prophets and Kings,* pp. 582-592.

[126] *Prophets and Kings,* pp. 589, 590.

[127] On the other hand, many do stand in jeopardy in the judgment. They are those who have "sins remaining upon the books of records, unrepented of and unforgiven" (*The Great Controversy,* p. 483). Unjustified before, they are not justified now. Heaven blots their names out of the books of record (*Ibid.,* pp. 486-488). Even for true believers the judgment is a time of special solemnity. The one essential is sorrow for sin and true repentance—only so can they be without "spot, or wrinkle, or any such thing."

[128] *Ibid.,* p. 425.

[129] *Testimonies,* vol. 2, p. 355; *Early Writings,* pp. 43, 44, 58, 279.

[130] "The Need of Educational Reform," *Testimonies,* vol. 6, pp. 129-131.

[131] Letter 126, 1898 (in *The SDA Bible Commentary,* Ellen G. White Comments, vol. 7, p. 968).

[132] Manuscript 85, 1903 (in *The SDA Bible Commentary,* Ellen G. White Comments, vol. 6, p. 1055).

[133] *The Great Controversy,* p. 613; *Early Writings,* pp. 48, 71, 279; *Testimonies,* vol. 5, p. 212; *Testimonies,* pp. 446, 510; *The SDA Bible Commentary,* Ellen G. White Comments, vol. 7, p. 981.

[134] *The Great Controversy,* p. 425.

[135] Ephesians 5:27 and Revelation 14:1-5, which Mrs. White quoted to say that the last-day believers must be spotless and without guile, have Old Testament roots in the promises of Psalms 15; 32:1, 2; and Zephaniah 3:13.

After 1888 Mrs. White applied Malachi 3:1-3 not only to God's people in the

HOW LONG, O LORD?

last days but also to Christ's cleansing the Temple in Jerusalem (see *The Desire of Ages*, [1898], p. 161) and to the work He desires to do in every human heart (see *The SDA Bible Commentary*, Ellen G. White Comments, vol. 5, pp. 1181, 1182, quoting from *The Southern Watchman*, Feb. 7, 1905, and *Prophets and Kings* [1917], p. 715).

[136] *Counsels to Parents and Teachers*, p. 321.

[137] "Walking in the Light," *Review and Herald*, Oct. 25, 1881, p. 257.

[138] *Testimonies*, vol. 8, pp. 36, 37, 252.

[139] *Ibid.*, vol. 9, p. 25.

[140] *Ibid.*, vol. 3, p. 94.

[141] *The SDA Encyclopedia*, pp. 43, 44.

[142] *Testimonies*, vol. 5, p. 460.

[143] "The Work for This Time," *Ibid.* (1900), vol. 6, p. 22; "The Day of the Lord Is Near, and Hasteth Greatly," *Review and Herald*, Nov. 24, 1904, p. 16; "Preparing for Christ's Return," *Review and Herald*, Nov. 12, 1914, p. 22.

[144] "Let the Trumpet Give a Certain Sound," *Review and Herald*, Dec. 6, 1892, p. 754 (in *Testimonies*, vol. 6, p. 18); *Selected Messages*, book 2, pp. 117, 118.

[145] *Education*, p. 184; see also Manuscript 9, 1891.

[146] "Advice to the Young," *Testimonies* (1889), vol. 5, pp. 525, 587.

[147] E. G. White to Dr. J. H. Kellogg, Mar. 2, 1895, written from New South Wales (in *Fundamentals of Christian Education*, pp. 334-367).

[148] *Fundamentals of Christian Education*, p. 368.

[149] Letter 25, 1902 (in *Medical Ministry*, p. 268).

[150] Manuscript 127, 1901 (in *Evangelism*, p. 378). See also "Labors in California," *Review and Herald*, Feb. 12, 1901, p. 97, where she defended spending $6,000 for her home at Elmshaven by saying she needed a suitable place to do her work. Actually she had used the gain on the sale of her home in Australia to make loans to the institutions there.

[151] "The Increase of Facilities," *Testimonies*, vol. 6, pp. 440, 441; Letter 25, 1902.

[152] Letter 25, 1902 (in *Medical Ministry*, p. 268).

[153] *Testimonies*, vol. 6, p. 478.

[154] "Preparing for Christ's Return," *Review and Herald*, Nov. 12, 1914, p. 21.

[155] *The Acts of the Apostles*, p. 431.

[156] *Fundamentals of Christian Education*, p. 547.

[157] *Testimonies*, vol. 5, p. 81.

[158] *The New Scofield Reference Bible*, ed. E. I. Scofield (New York: Oxford University Press, 1967).

[159] Frederick Dale Bruner, *A Theology of the Holy Spirit; The Pentecostal Experience and the New Testament Witness* (Grand Rapids: Eerdmans, 1970), p. 28.

[160] *The Great Controversy*, pp. 611, 612.

[161] *The Desire of Ages*, pp. 234, 235; *The Great Controversy*, pp. 347, 348.

[162] *Spiritual Gifts: The Great Controversy Between Christ and His Angels and Satan and His Angels* (Battle Creek, Mich.: Steam Press, 1858).

[163] *Steps to Christ, Thoughts From the Mount of Blessing, The Ministry of Healing*, and *Christ's Object Lessons*.

[164] Letter, Nov. 10, 1844, in *The Midnight Cry*, Dec. 5, 1844, p. 180.

[165] "Eschatology," *Twentieth Century Theology in the Making* (New York: Harper and Row, Fontana Books, 1969), vol. 1, pp. 289, 290.

[166] Beatrice S. Neall, *The Concept of Character in the Apocalypse* (Washington, D.C.: University Press of America, 1983), pp. 99, 100. This book is a careful study of the ethics of the book of Revelation.

CHAPTER IV

The Delay of Christ's Coming

In this chapter we will define the concept of delay as Mrs. White used it at different times of her life, note its relationship to the three angels' messages of Revelation 14, learn the reasons she gave for it, and analyze how she employed it in her exhortations.

Her earliest statements on a possible delay appeared about 14 years after the 1844 disappointment. While she had written in 1849 that time was short and that "very soon" God would decide every case for life or for death,[1] in 1858 she said that Jesus could not come yet because the believers must yet "suffer for Jesus and endure greater trials. They must give up errors and traditions received from men, and turn wholly to God and His word. They must be purified, made white, and tried."[2]

Here we see Christ waiting for the spiritual experience of the Advent believers, but in the rest of the book she describes a sequence of events not tied to the spiritual progress of the church. Christ, she wrote, went into the Most Holy Place of the heavenly sanctuary in 1844 to make a special atonement for Israel, receive the kingdom from His Father, and then return to earth to take His people. Then she described the three angel's messages, the time of trouble, and the actual advent of Christ to deliver His people. She said He is waiting for the spiritual improvement of His people, but she also said that He is waiting to finish His own work in heaven. He would make the special atonement, receive the kingdom, and *then* return to earth.

HOW LONG, O LORD?

Her 1858 statement was related to the new emphasis on the message to the church in Laodicea (Rev. 3:14-22) that James White introduced in 1856. Adventists had expected the Lord to return within a few years after 1844, and by the mid-1850s began to ask why He had not yet arrived. In 1856 James suggested the Laodicean message as a possible reason, and many of the believers agreed.[3] Mrs. White supported his interpretation in two articles published in 1857 and another in 1859.[4] In the latter she recalled that when Adventist believers first applied the Laodicean message to themselves, "nearly all believed that this message would end in the loud cry of the third angel," but she continued that "if the message had been of as short duration as many of us supposed, there would have been no time for them to develop character." She had indeed believed that Christ would come in a very few years, for she wrote that the message was designed to arouse the people of God and lead them to zealous repentance that they might be fitted for the loud cry of the third angel. By 1858, however, the Lord told her that the hoped-for revival would not come quickly or easily.[5]

Some Adventists have concluded from her statements in volume 1 of *Testimonies,* pages 186 and 187, that the Lord could have come by 1859 if the church had completely accepted the Laodicean message. The sentence "God has given the message time to do its work," they claim, shows that the three years were enough to accomplish the needed reformation. But such an interpretation overlooks the task of preaching to the world. By 1859 the Adventists still had no concept of taking their message beyond the northeastern United States. Their membership in 1867 was only 4,320,[6] and it would have been much less in 1857. Proclaiming their appointed message to the *world* in three years would have required a miracle in communications beyond anything ever seen in the history of the church.

THE DELAY OF CHRIST'S COMING

As a matter of fact, time was not the main point of her articles. She sought to convince her readers that the testimony to the Laodiceans applied to them, and the reason it has not produced a greater result was the hardness of their hearts. Her evangelistic burden was uppermost, as always, rather than the time of Jesus' return.

Commenting on Mark 13:35 and Luke 12:35, Mrs. White rebuked worldliness in the church in 1868. Quoting the Mark passage, she wrote, "The Lord intimates a delay before the morning finally dawns," and added, "He would not have them give way to weariness, . . . because the morning does not open upon them as soon as they expected." The evidence is ambiguous, however. The faithful ones were waiting in the third watch of the night. Therefore there could be but a little period left: "Now the period of waiting is necessarily shorter than at first." Yet she also stated that "the morning is deferred in mercy, because if the Master should come, so many would be found unready. God's unwillingness to have His people perish has been the reason for so long delay." Thus she refers to both a fixed time ("the period of waiting is necessarily shorter than at first"), and also a delay.

Ellen White thus used two different hammers to pound the same nail. Living in the third watch called for threefold earnestness. She urged the believers to be in the "watching" position, which meant to turn from earthly pleasure and riches, and glory rather in tribulation, affliction, and necessities.[7]

In 1876 Mrs. White referred to God's infinite mercy as a reason for the delay when she commented on the days of Noah. The world had more time for repentance, but because of it sinners flattered themselves that He would never come.[8] The reference to Noah indicates that God had set the time of Christ's return far enough in the future that sinners would have plenty of time to repent, but it does not mean that His plan had been altered because of His mercy. Even this kind of statement points to nearness within the generation alive at the time, for no one has more than his own lifetime in which to repent. The generation alive in 1876 could receive no benefit from time extending beyond their own death.

During the first half of Ellen White's ministry we find few statements that "delay" meant a postponement of God's plans. As the years passed, however, she naturally spoke more often about it. A few weeks after her husband died in 1881, she wrote poignantly of God's purpose in the waiting time. If it seemed long and if "bowed by affliction and worn with toil, we feel impatient for our commission to close," we must remember that God left us on earth to encounter conflicts, perfect Christian character, and win many souls to Christ.[9]

She used the parable of the ten virgins also to reveal God's purpose in the delay. Just as the bridegroom's delay tested the maidens, the apparent delay of Christ tested the church. She told believers to make sure they had the oil of the Spirit. Each must fall on the Rock, Christ Jesus, and permit the old nature to be broken up.[10] It was a general spiritual application of the parable.

In the book *The Great Controversy*, however, Ellen White employed it in the old Millerite sense. The delay of the bridegroom symbolized the passing of the time in the spring of 1844. The cry at midnight was the August proclamation that the Lord would come on October 22. When Christ did not appear, they found an answer in Luke 12:36, that they must wait for the master to *come home* from the wedding feast.[11] It is clear that Mrs. White could use the parable as a hammer to pound more than one nail.[12]

Because of the apparent extension of time, she saw believers in danger of becoming careless in words and actions. They must use the time to overcome defects in

THE DELAY OF CHRIST'S COMING

their characters and help others to see the beauty of holiness.[13] She had pointed to such a danger as early as 1849, when she wrote that because time had continued a few years longer than some expected (even then!), they concluded it might extend a few years more, and in this way their minds drifted away from the truth and out after the world.[14] In each case her evangelistic burden was apparent, but her attitude toward a literal delay was ambiguous.

Human Perceptions of Delay

When we speak of "delay," we are referring to two different questions. We can ask on one hand, "Has God actually changed His plan and postponed the coming of Christ?" Or we can inquire, "Does it merely seem like a delay to us because we do not know the time?" To a 4-year-old child waiting for Christmas the holiday seems long delayed, but there is no real deferment unless his parents decide to celebrate it on January 25. Henry Lummis, one of the speakers gathered for the Prophetic Bible Conference in New York in 1878, was correct when he said that we are little skilled in celestial arithmetic.[15]

The Millerites thought there was a delay in the spring of 1844, which was the original time of expectation.[16] When the Lord did not appear they found comfort in Habakkuk 2:3, which seemed to predict their experience. It showed that "the vision of time did not tarry, though it had seemed to do so." What seemed like delay was not really so.

Mrs. White borrowed the language of Habakkuk 2:3 again in 1890 to say there has been a seeming delay ever since the days of Abraham, but added, "at the appointed time 'it will surely come, it will not tarry.'"[17] The promise to Abraham will have its fulfillment when Christ returns. The world still waits, but the inheritance will be given at the time God has set.

HOW LONG, O LORD?

In 1900 she found another reason for the seeming delay in 2 Peter 3:9—the Lord was not willing that any should perish, but that all should come to repentance.[18]

Mrs. White writes in similar terms about the apparent delays of both the first and second advents of Christ. Adam and Eve hoped their first son might be the promised deliverer—"but the fulfillment of the promise tarried." Century after century passed away, and many expressed their disappointment in the words of Ezekiel 12:22—"The days are prolonged, and every vision faileth." Everyone thought the promise postponed, but Galatians 4:4 showed that "God's purposes know no haste and no delay."[19]

It is clear, therefore, that she knew all about apparent delays owing to disappointed expectations, but we have not yet been able to answer the question whether there has been a literal change in God's date for the last day. Before we can do so, we must consider another type of "delay" revealed in her comments on the parable of the wicked servant (Matthew 24:48 and Luke 12:45). Here the question is neither a perceived nor an actual delay, but a willful attitude that shows itself in evil deeds.

The Wicked Servant Who Says, "My Master Is Delayed"

In the early years after 1844 Ellen White herself sometimes faced the accusation that she was the evil servant who said the Lord's coming was delayed, because she refused to accept any new dates.[20] Later she applied the text to others. In the 1870s she wrote that faith in the soon coming of Christ had begun to wane in the church. The members were saying, "My Lord delayeth His coming," by their words, their works, and their lives. They loved money and had little of the spirit of sacrifice.[21]

During the 1880s she warned against loving the world. Satan was leading men to "put off the evil day and become

THE DELAY OF CHRIST'S COMING

in spirit like the world, imitating its customs."[22] It was the man of selfish, worldly spirit who said in his heart, "My Lord delayeth His coming."[23] He lacked the "true advent spirit."[24]

All who believed in the soon coming of Christ would demonstrate it by holy living and diligent witnessing. One who considered it delayed would show so by sin. It is the *wicked* servant who says in his heart that the master is delayed. In one case Mrs. White rebuked a prominent leader's wife in these words:

> I saw that for some time past, Sister J has had a rebellious spirit, has been self-willed. . . . I saw that she did not bring the coming of the Lord as near as she should, and that her mind, instead of being at Rochester, should be all swallowed up in the work of God, and she should be seeking opportunities to help her husband, to hold up his hands, and to labor wherever there was an opportunity.[25]

Very early she also wrote: "Many among us put off the coming of the Lord too far, and their works correspond with their faith."[26]

Around 1900 she observed that those who said the Lord delayed His coming had ceased to cooperate with God in the salvation of others. The doctrine of the soon coming of Christ was a means to an end: namely, to prepare people for the final judgment.[27] Ministers who hovered over the churches, neglecting to take the Adventist message to those who had not heard it, received a rebuke for saying that the Lord had delayed His coming.[28] Thus, both the nearness of Christ's coming and also the warning against saying that it tarried she used as motivations for witnessing.

An 1894 article by her linked the ideas of a fixed time for the end, a literal delay by the Lord, and a stubborn desire for delay on the part of the sinner. She said that each week counted one less to the appointed time of the judgment, but also asked why the Lord so long postponed

His coming, for the whole host of heaven waited to fulfill the last work for the world. She answered that the few who professed to believe had not become burning lights in the world—they were saying in their hearts that their Master was delayed.[29]

The article clearly shows that she had much more concern for spiritual preparations than for time. Here she speaks of an appointed time for the judgment and also of a delay. Both serve as hammers pounding the same nail. Both stemmed from the time prophecies on one side and the three angels' messages on the other. God had an appointed time for the coming of Christ, but the three angels laid out the task to be done first. The prophecies showed the sovereignty of God while the three angels reminded of man's responsibility.

Belief in nearness, according to Ellen White, leads to holiness, but the idea of delay distracts the believer into sin. For her it was not enough to believe that Christ is coming sometime—we must believe He is coming soon. She used both the nearness and the apparent delay to make His return real to the life of the church.

Increasing Clarity

We have seen that Ellen White's list of future events pointed to a fixed time for Christ's coming. In 1888 she wrote:

> I have ever had one testimony to bear: The Lord will not come at that period, and you [date-setters] are weakening the faith of even Adventists, and fastening the world in their unbelief. There have been plainly set before me events of great and thrilling interest, which must transpire before Christ will come. Satan will move mightily from beneath, and will delude the world, while the Lord God Omnipotent will move from above and prepare a people to stand in the great day of His wrath.[30]

Seen from this standpoint, it would appear that she

recognized no delay in the appointed time for Christ to return. But when we look at it from the standpoint of the task that believers must accomplish and the character they must develop, then we can speak of delay.

In 1883 Mrs. White took the clear position on delay that she held through the rest of her life alongside the conviction of the nearness of Christ's coming.[31] In a defense of her statements on the Second Advent, she wrote that the promises and threatenings of God are alike conditional, and that Christ could have come if all the Advent believers in 1844-1848 had united in proclaiming the message of the third angel. She compared their experience to the delay of the Israelites' entrance into Canaan under Moses and Joshua.[32] Here she spoke of an actual delay, a postponement, of Christ's return.

Mrs. White was replying to a booklet by A. C. Long, of Marion, Iowa, charging her with suppressing certain statements from her early works when she republished them in *Early Writings*. Long charged that she no longer believed those ideas. He also accused her of being a false prophet because of her 1849 statement, "I saw that the time for Jesus to be in the Most Holy Place was nearly finished, and that time cannot last but a very little longer."[33] (He slightly misquoted her. Actually she had written, "Time can last but a very little longer.") Since "nearly finished" could not mean less than half done, Long argued, Christ should have come by 1854.

Long was a member of the Marion Party, a dissident Adventist group started in 1866 by B. F. Snook and W. H. Brinkerhoff, first president and secretary of the Iowa Conference. After the constituency replaced Snook with George I. Butler in 1865, Snook established headquarters at Marion, Iowa. Later the group moved to Stanberry, Missouri, as the Church of God (Adventist).

Church leaders in Battle Creek prepared a careful reply to Long's pamphlet, which appeared in a 16-page *Supple-*

ment to the *Review and Herald,* Aug. 14, 1883. Butler himself wrote "A Brief History of the 'Marion' Movement," pages 7, 8, and "The Visions: How They Are Held Among S. D. Adventists," pages 11, 12. Ellen White's own reply did not see publication in her lifetime,[34] but J. H. Waggoner included several of its distinctive ideas in his article "'Suppression,' and 'The Shut Door,'" pages 1-3 of the *Review and Herald Supplement.*

In her statement Mrs. White wrote that she could no more be accused of falsehood because time had continued longer than her testimony indicated than could Christ and His disciples. Quoting 1 Corinthians 7:29, 30; Romans 13:12; Revelation 1:3; and 22:6, 7, she said they had also pictured time as being short. The angels of God in their messages to men had always depicted the time before Christ's return as brief—thus it had always been presented to her. The Lord had not appeared as soon as they hoped, but she never entertained the possibility that His word had failed. The questions critical scholars were asking—whether Christ or the early church was wrong in His or their apocalyptic faith—did not concern her.

Then she said that the word of the Lord had not failed, for "the promises and threatenings of God are alike conditional." The requirements were that God's people must proclaim the third angel's message, that the believers must turn their attention to Christ's work in the heavenly sanctuary, that the Sabbath reform must be carried forward, and that the people of God must "purify their souls through obedience to the truth, and be prepared to stand without fault before Him at His coming." Her reply, then, was that Christ waited for the piety and witness of the church, and the members had not yet met the conditions.

Here Mrs. White definitely has in mind a real postponement of the coming of Christ. If the first-day Adventists after the disappointment in 1844 had accepted the

THE DELAY OF CHRIST'S COMING

seventh-day Sabbath reform and helped proclaim it to the world, the Lord would have "wrought mightily" with them to finish the task, and Christ would have returned to take His people home. As it was, the majority opposed the few who received the third angel's message, "the work was hindered, and the world was left in darkness." If the *whole* body had accepted the new message, their history—indeed, the history of the world—would have been different. The failure of Adventists to accept the Sabbath postponed the end of all things.

Mrs. White never made statements about the past or future without applying them to the present, however. The early first-day Adventists may have delayed the Lord in the 1840s, but she spoke to the present by pointing to the "unbelief, the worldliness, unconsecration, and strife" among her own people as the reason they were still in the world. The sins of God's people had forced a delay in His plan. "It was not the will of God that the coming of Christ should be thus delayed," she wrote, no more than it was God's plan that His ancient people should wander 40 years in the wilderness. The same sins that kept them out of the promised land had "delayed the entrance of modern Israel into the heavenly Canaan."

We have noted in Chapter III that Ellen White always warned against setting dates, and while others use her early statements to do so, she never did herself. She said the Lord might come in one or two years, or He might not come for 20.[35] Thus she allowed time for the ordinary activities of life, such as marriage and home, but still maintained her ethical appeal. Her stance dealt more with the believer's obligations than with a chronological calculation.

Long's criticism took Ellen White's 1849 statement and used it to set the date 1854. Since Christ did not come then, he accused her of being a false prophet. He tied her words to the calendar more closely than she intended.

HOW LONG, O LORD?

Consistent in decrying all dates, she detached her statements from the calendar by saying Christ's advent was both near and delayed.

In her attitude Mrs. White agreed with that of the Prophetic Bible Conference that had met five years earlier in New York. Quoting 2 Peter 3:12 (margin), the common declaration of that conference said that by watching, praying, working, waiting, and preaching in all the world Christians could hasten the arrival of the day of God.[36] While she herself did not quote the marginal reading of this verse until 1898,[37] she agreed that Christ was waiting on the piety and witness of the church. She went beyond the conference position in reasoning that if the church has a mission to finish before Christ can come, then the church is responsible for the delay.

Two possible reasons kept the Bible conference in 1878 from going as far as she did. One is that they did not have the conviction of being a people with the last warning message for the world. They were not a unified group in any case, belonging to a variety of denominations, and none of them believed they were fulfilling prophecy as Adventists did. Another reason was that Darbyite dispensationalism, which emphasized the every-moment expectancy of the rapture so strongly that it could not speak of delay, gradually took over the Bible conference movement. "Delay" means that we know something about time, but dispensationalists held that the Lord had said nothing about the date of the rapture.

Mrs. White, however, had to deal with delay as the years lengthened after 1844. We have noted that she wrote somewhat ambiguously in her early years. In her first comments (in 1864) on Israel's rebellion at Kadesh-Barnea, she gave a simple exposition of the text without making any comparison with modern Israel's failure,[38] but in 1883 she did make the connection. And thus she said that human sins had thwarted God's will.

THE DELAY OF CHRIST'S COMING

How then does her 1883 position on delay fit into her overall eschatology? We have seen in Chapter II that she based her faith in the nearness of Christ's coming on time prophecies that climaxed in 1844 and were summarized in the three angels' messages. Now we see that her 1883 position on delay goes back to the same root:

> God had committed to His people a work to be accomplished on earth. The third angel's message was to be given. . . . The message must be proclaimed with a loud voice. . . . The people of God must purify their souls through obedience to the truth, and be prepared to stand without fault before Him at His coming.[39]

During the first 39 years of her ministry, Ellen White held that the three angels' messages predicted a revival and therefore must be proclaimed *because* the Lord was coming soon. In her last 32 years she added that the revival must come and messages be proclaimed *so that* the Lord could come.[40] During the latter period she wrote of both nearness and delay, the sovereignty of God and the responsibility of man. The root of both was the prophecy of Revelation 14.

In the 1883 document we find the chief points of her eschatological thought through her later years. Many times she repeated the statement that the Lord could have returned if the church had met certain conditions. Just as soon as the people of God were sealed in their foreheads and thus prepared for the shaking, then Jesus would return.[41] Sometimes the condition the church must satisfy consisted of developing the character in Christ's image; other times it involved preaching the Adventist message to the world. She compared church members to soldiers who had not done their duty, and to the 10 virgins who all should have proclaimed the truth, but because five were foolish, the work did not get done. Mrs. White urged Adventists to give of their money to spread the church's message. Because they had not done their duty, the work was far behind what it should have been.[42]

In most of these statements Mrs. White wrote in the negative: that is, she told what would have been if—but it did not happen. Twice, however, she used a true-to-fact condition. Once she said that if the church had its army of young rightly trained, they could soon carry the message to the whole world, and the Lord would come. Another time she stated that when the members do their work at home and abroad, the world will soon be warned and the Lord will return.[43] Both approaches urged the same thing: that believers should live holy lives and be diligent witnesses.

Mrs. White repeated her comparison between ancient and modern Israel, found in the 1883 document, only in *Spirit of Prophecy*, volume 4, and in *The Great Controversy*.[44] It did not continue to play a prominent part in her eschatology. The constant nearness of the Advent had always been in her thoughts, but until 1883 she had never before spelled it out so clearly. In this document she crystallized latent ideas to meet the critic's challenge and at the same time provided a rationale for the delayed Advent, which she used repeatedly from that time on. However, neither her statement that God and His agents have always represented time as short nor the idea that the promises and threatenings of God are alike conditional was published in her lifetime.

Taylor Grant Bunch (1885-1969), prominent Adventist leader who pastored large churches and taught religion at Atlantic Union College and Loma Linda University, duplicated a series of vesper sermons in 1937 entitled "The Exodus and Advent Movements" that held that the Adventist Church is repeating the experiences of ancient Israel. He concluded that the 1888 General Conference session on righteousness by faith was the turning point when the church rejected God's leading and therefore put

THE DELAY OF CHRIST'S COMING

off entering the heavenly Canaan. By collecting many Ellen White statements denouncing those who opposed the 1888 message, Elder Bunch built up his thesis that the church had postponed the coming of Christ and had turned back to the wilderness.

Bunch depended heavily on *The Great Controversy*, pages 457, 458, perhaps not knowing that she had first written the passage in 1883. Furthermore, he included few statements made after 1903, when, with the 1888 crisis behind her, Mrs. White took a more optimistic view of the church. It is doubtful, therefore, that she would have supported his basic thesis.

Another leader who thought 1888 was a pivotal year in the experience of Adventists was Leroy Edwin Froom (1890-1974), teacher, editor, author, and secretary of the Ministerial Association of the General Conference. In his *Movement of Destiny*, pages 570-582, he also built most of his case on Mrs. White's 1883 statement. He believed that if the church as a whole had accepted Jones's and Waggoner's corrections of its faulty theology, it would have opened the door for Christ to come, but Ellen White did not say that.

She had been greatly concerned about final events before 1888, giving one chapter to the subject in 1882 and two in 1885,[45] but the reason for her concern was the enforcement of Sunday laws. At the 1888 General Conference session itself she made only one passing reference to the nearness of Christ's coming: "Now, brethren, we are almost home; we shall soon hear the voice of the Saviour richer than any music, saying, Your warfare is accomplished."[46]

After the 1888 session she referred to righteousness by faith just once in connection with the final events:

> The time of test is just upon us, for the loud cry of the third angel has already begun in the revelation of the righteousness of Christ, the sin-pardoning Redeemer. This

HOW LONG, O LORD?

is the beginning of the light of the angel whose glory shall fill the whole earth.[47]

The thrust of the article is that because the signs were multiplying, believers must search the Scriptures, warn the people, and accept the gift of Christ's righteousness. The emphasis, as usual, is on the exhortation, not the time.

While this one statement connects the issue of righteousness by faith to the nearness of Christ's coming, none of her comments on delay that she modeled on the 1883 document ever mention it. The Sunday law problem in 1888 pointed to Christ's coming much more than did the emphasis on righteousness by faith.

The idea of hastening the advent of Christ began to appear in her writings in 1898. She pictured the immense suffering that sin has caused God and wrote that "in order to destroy sin and its results He gave His best Beloved, and He has put it in our power, through cooperation with Him, to bring this scene of misery to an end," followed by a quotation of Matthew 24:14.[48] In this way she made the witnesses of the gospel the fulcrum of world history and left the way open for the implication that Christians shoulder blame for the continuation of suffering in the world. She did not take the thought that far herself, however, saying only that the witnesses can help end the suffering. Her concept of hastening was in harmony with her conviction that the last days began in 1844; she applied 2 Peter 3:12 and all "last days" admonitions to her own time.

The Message to Be Given

Mrs. White called the three angels' messages both a warning and a winning message, just as Noah's proclamation was. For those who came into the ark it was a message of salvation, but for those who refused, it brought condemnation. In the same way, the Adventist

THE DELAY OF CHRIST'S COMING

message will be a "savor of life unto life to all who accept it, and of condemnation to all who reject it." We have a message of hope for those perishing in ignorance.[49] Our work is that of a man who warns his neighbor that his house is on fire. Mrs. White was always more concerned to get the warning to the neighbor than to calculate when the roof would collapse.

She believed that every converted person will take the announcement of Jesus' soon coming to the world. Everyone who has received the light will zealously share it with others.[50] God can display the knowledge of His will and the wonders of His grace only through human witnesses. He will not pour out His Spirit in the latter rain while the largest portion of the church are not laborers with Him.[51] If every one of the church members were a living missionary, she wrote in an echo of the 1883 statement, the work would soon be done.[52]

Seventh-day Adventism had to proclaim its message to the entire world, although it took time to grasp this fact. It was a generation after 1844 before it sent out its first missionary. During Mrs. White's years in Europe (1885-1887) and Australia (1891-1900) she urged the believers in America to think of foreign countries. They were not to localize their work but give the Word in all cities and villages, highways and byways. From Europe she spoke of nearness: "Our time to work is short, and there is a world to be warned." But she felt that evangelism there was going far more slowly than God would have it.[53] The size of the task and the fact that workers were few showed that the Lord could not come within a year or two. The nearness of His return was only a motive to be earnest in the work.

In 1906 Mrs. White said that her understanding of the work to be done had enlarged through the years. She wrote they had thought it would have been finished before then, but "light came from the Lord regarding the extension of the work." After quoting Matthew 28:18,19, she said, "Then we understood that there was a world to be warned." The message was to go to "every city in America" and in the "regions beyond."[54] She always called the church to "do more, *never less*" until the Lord's work should encircle the world. The only boundary must be the farthest horizon.[55]

She found Bible evidence that the Lord is waiting for the gospel proclamation in Matthew 24:14. "It will not tarry past the time that the message is borne to all nations, tongues, and peoples."[56] Unlike the Millerites and modern Adventists, however, she did not count missionaries, languages, or countries entered. Another support text was Revelation 7:1-4, which pictures the four angels holding the winds of final trouble to give the believers time to warn the world.[57]

So deep was her conviction after 1883 that Christ was waiting for the church that she once wrote we might have to remain in the world many more years because of insubordination, but in that case we were not to blame God for the consequence of our own sins.[58]

This often-quoted statement appears in a letter of encouragement to the founder of another struggling institution. Percy Magan had moved Battle Creek College to Berrien Springs, Michigan, in July, 1901, and had been doing the work of several men in getting it established in its new location. He faced opposition from the leaders in Battle Creek, little money, a divided faculty, and no college buildings. He had suffered an attack of typhoid fever in 1900 and a relapse in 1901 that left him with myocardial complications.[59]

Along with the encouragement, she urged Magan to take a rest. She aimed the charge of insubordination at the leaders who opposed him, but he could not expect to heal the hurt because of their failure. He must make haste slowly: the Lord would not be pleased if he took on so

THE DELAY OF CHRIST'S COMING

many projects that it broke his strength. She wrote: "I cannot tell you what you should do, but I can tell you what not to do: Do not worry, be not unbelieving, and do not think that you can blossom into a perfect school at its very planting on new soil."

In her comments that the Lord was waiting for His church to act, she did not mean that He had abdicated His sovereignty. The work is always *His* work. It is His mercy that delays the end so that more may be saved. He has given the church its task, but He remains in charge of it. The messages of Revelation 14 are the messages of *angels*, although given by men.

We find an important instance of the relationship between the sovereignty of God and the responsibility of man, between nearness and delay, in Mrs. White's comments on the Sunday-law crisis of the late 1880s. That threat was a fulfillment of what Adventists had been proclaiming for 40 years. The final crisis seemed to be at hand, but the church was not ready, neither in their personal experience nor in their evangelism of the world. She then urged the members to pray for a respite so they would have time to do their neglected work. Ellen White did not believe the time had fully come when Adventists would have their liberties restricted. The church must educate the public on the principles of freedom of religion and separation of church and state, but their responsibility included the entire work of the three angels. They must send missionaries to all parts of the world and proclaim the warning against disobeying the law of Jehovah.[60]

Why did Mrs. White think the time had not come for their liberties to end? They had been predicting this since the 1850s, but now she said it was happening too soon. As a consequence they must seek a respite, a delay. This fact modifies the statements she had made since 1883, that the end would not come until the church had finished its work on the earth. The final events now seemed to be starting even though the church had *not* done its work.

It is clear that her view of the nearness of Christ's coming as based on the Sunday-law crisis was affected by the task to be done. Church membership in 1889 was only 25,378 in the United States, with barely 2,000 elsewhere.[61] Since Adventists had not given the three angel's messages to the world, she reasoned that it must be God's will to put off the final crisis. Therefore she prayed for a delay, believing the time had not yet come for their liberties to cease. Both the nearness seen in the Sunday-law problem and the delay requested grew out of her understanding of the three angels.

As the Sunday issue faded during the 1890s, Ellen White wrote that God had granted the moment of respite.[62] She still spoke of nearness, however, for she said the signs were ominous. There must be no delay in sending the warning to all parts of the world. As a practical matter it is a long-term project to send missionaries to all parts of the world, but even as she urged the church to send them out she constantly emphasized the shortness of time. Always she felt the pressure to do the work now!

The People to Be Prepared

The Lord will have a pure and true people on earth when He comes, and He has not left the church wholly dependent on human leaders. If the shepherds are not true, Mrs. White wrote, He will take charge of the flock Himself.[63] They are the ones who will receive the seal of God, but they must remedy the defects in their characters beforehand. No one can receive it while he has one spot or stain. The spots she mentioned in one article were pride, passion, and spiritual slothfulness. Elsewhere she listed them as envy, evil-surmisings, and evil-speaking.[64] In fact, they included all her exhortations. She insisted that the work of overcoming sin must be done in this life: not

THE DELAY OF CHRIST'S COMING

one error of character will be removed when Christ shall come.[65]

God and man both have a part in developing a holy people. Heaven is active to make them ready on earth, but God also calls for men to prepare a people to stand in the day of the Lord.[66] God puts the seal on men who sigh and cry for the abominations done in the land, upon those who settle into the truth so they cannot be moved.

Speaking of this people raises the question whether she thought of a set number that must be reached before Christ can return. She hinted at the idea twice, once in connection with the work of the sanitariums: "Our sanitarium work is to help make up the number of God's people."[67] The second allusion involved the close of probation. At that time, she wrote, when Christ will have finished the atonement for His people and blotted out their sins, the number of His subjects will be made up.[68]

To these hints—they are only that—we may add her thoughts on the church as a temple.[69] The world, she wrote, is like a quarry from which stones are cut out to be placed in the temple. Although the first builders were martyred, yet the church grew—it slowly ascended as stone after stone was added. The work is not complete yet. We have our part to act in the construction also.

This illustration balances her harvest metaphor, in which she said,

> "When the fruit is brought forth, immediately he putteth in the sickle, because the harvest is come." Christ is waiting with longing desire for the manifestation of Himself in His church. When the character of Christ shall be perfectly reproduced in His people, then He will come to claim them as His own.
>
> It is the privilege of every Christian not only to look for but to hasten the coming of our Lord Jesus Christ (2 Peter 3:12, margin). Were all who profess His name bearing fruit to His glory, how quickly the whole world would be sown

with the seed of the gospel. Quickly the last great harvest would be ripened, and Christ would come to gather the precious grain.[70]

The harvest metaphor says that Christ will come when His people perfectly reproduce His character, but the temple metaphor implies that He will return when His church is complete. In all ages it is one temple. We might conclude that she thought of a set number of people required to make up the temple, but she does not make this point.

If she had intended us to understand that all we have to do is to convert a certain number of individuals and then the end will happen, she could have made it clear, but her statements never became that mathematical. What is obvious is our constant duty to help build the people of God. Her comments about numbers remain only hints.

There is one other area of Ellen White's thought that we might possibly read as pointing to a predetermined number of the redeemed. It appears in her comments on the 144,000 of Revelation 7:1-8 and 14:1-5 who follow the Lamb wherever He goes. In the account of her first vision she pictures them as the ones who will be translated at Christ's coming without dying. The number then seemed to be literal. She put no special emphasis on it, however, using it only as a designation for the faithful ones who will survive the time of trouble, not as an announcement of how many God will save.

In her later references to the 144,000 she focused on their spiritual character, and the significance of the exact number faded even farther from view.[71] Finally she developed a present-day application and made direct appeals to put away iniquity and keep the commandments of God. She wrote that God has a people on earth who follow the Lamb wherever He goes, and those who expect to do so in the courts above must follow Him here.[72]

THE DELAY OF CHRIST'S COMING

The Limit of God's Mercy

Any eschatology rooted in the three angel's messages has to give a prominent place to the wrath of God. Ellen White wrote that God keeps an account of the sins of individuals, families, and nations, and there is a limit beyond which He can no longer exercise mercy. When the accumulated figures in His records mark the sum of transgression complete, then "wrath will come, unmixed with mercy, and then it will be seen what a tremendous thing it is to have worn out the divine patience." The crisis will result when the nations unite to make void God's law—a clear reference to the Sunday controversy current at that time.[73]

The concept that God has a prescribed limit for wickedness assumes that the world is a corporate body through all ages. Men have been filling their cup of iniquity for centuries, she wrote, and all through history sinners have been treasuring up wrath against the day of wrath.[74] Each generation has been adding to the total.

This could lead to the idea that the last generation suffers for the sins of their fathers. However, she qualified this in her discussion of Jerusalem's fate by saying that children do not stand condemned for their parents' sins, but when they know all the light given to their parents and reject the added light given to themselves, they become partakers of their parents' sins and complete the measure of their iniquity.[75] Thus she held both a corporate and an individual view of sin.

What do her thoughts on the total of sins imply about the delay of Christ's coming? The evidence is mixed. On one hand she held that God is keeping the records open as long as possible, not willing that any should perish.[76] But on the other, she used the same facts to point to the nearness of Christ's return and urge the church to proclaim the warning. The "rapidly swelling figures show that the time for God's visitations has nearly come"—

therefore believers should "labor diligently to save others."⁷⁷ The increasing wickedness was a sign that urged men to heed and follow the Lord in self-denying service.⁷⁸ Once again we find her uniting nearness and delay in her pastoral appeals.

Summary and Reflections

We have seen that when Ellen White referred to the time of Christ's coming in the first half of her ministry she spoke mainly of nearness and a definite date known only to God. But after 1883 she wrote more clearly of delay, while continuing to speak also of nearness.

This addition to her thought appeared in a document she composed in response to criticism that she had been a false prophet in writing of the soon return of Christ in 1849. In her reply she commented for the first time that the New Testament had also predicted that Christ would come soon—the angels had always represented it so—and her position was just the same.

She went on to say that Christ had been delayed by the failure of early Adventists to accept the third angel's message and by sins among her own people, just as Israel had waited for 40 years before entering Canaan. Fifteen years later she added that they could hasten the advent of Christ by holy living and diligent witnessing. The time of the end, therefore, depended on the life and work of Seventh-day Adventists.

These concepts have given Adventists their broad vision and sense of mission. Standing in the last days as Elijah and John the Baptist did in their day, Adventists believe they have an essential part to play in the final drama. Christians have always been motivated by gratitude for Christ's sacrifice and love for God and men, but Adventists also respond to the conviction that they are giving the *last* call to prepare men for the end. Seldom has anyone had stronger reasons for holy living and diligent

THE DELAY OF CHRIST'S COMING

witnessing. Such a conviction is a natural development from the prophetic principles that Ellen White inherited from the Millerites and the Puritans. One could accuse the little church of delusions of grandeur, until we remember that Christ started with only 12.

Several questions surface, however, as we try to relate the themes of nearness and delay. The Bible has delay parables, but they do not teach that human beings cause it. The bridegroom of Matthew 25 tarried, but not because of the sleeping virgins. The householder who left his property with his servants came back after a long time (Matthew 25:14-30), but his return was not contingent on their faithfulness. The reappearance of the high priest from the Most Holy Place on the Day of Atonement was not dependent on the worship of the people in the court (Leviticus 16:20).

Ellen White read more than the parables, however. Such texts as Matthew 24:14, Revelation 7:1-4, and 14:6-12 showed that Christ waits for the witness of His people. "This gospel of the kingdom shall be preached in all the world for a witness unto all nations; and *then* shall the end come."

Nevertheless, the meaning of this passage is not as clear as it seems. What is the world? Is it only the world of today? What about those who died yesterday? Preaching the gospel to the world is not a task one can complete in the way he finishes reaping 100 acres of wheat. The world exists in time as well as space. The boundaries of the wheat field keep moving. People are always being born and always dying. What then does it mean to preach the gospel to all the world? Is it a frantic effort to reach every living person within a certain number of years, ignoring those who have slipped into their graves?

Unfortunately, Mrs. White did not deal with this question. She wrote that those who live in the last days have the possibility and responsibility of finishing the task so the Lord can return, but her greatest emphasis was on the believers' obligation to be continually at it.

As we think of the apparent delay in Christ's coming, we sometimes assume that we know exactly why He has not come yet. We would do well, however, to heed her warning in an 1891 sermon: "It Is Not for You to Know the Times and the Seasons."[79] God has told us many of the factors that govern the time of Christ's return, but can we be sure He has revealed everything to us? Do we really know all the conditions? It could be that in His sovereignty God has others that He has not shared with us. The times and the seasons remain in *His* hand. The *secret* things still belong to the Lord our God.

While Ellen White wrote much about the work that Seventh-day Adventists must do, we need to look at her attitude toward other churches also. In *The Great Controversy* she saw the Lord at work among the early Christians persecuted by pagan and papal Rome, then among the Waldenses, Wycliffe, Huss, Jerome, Luther, Calvin, Wesley, and the Pilgrims who came to America.

But she believed the Protestant churches of America and Europe failed to continue the Reformation. Their religion had degenerated into formalism, and before long they had almost as great a need of reform as had the Roman Church of Luther's time. The influence of the Spirit was narrowed down to a small remnant of faithful ones.

In her own day, of course, she believed God had certainly been at work among the Millerites and the Seventh-day Adventists, but when the other churches rejected the message of Jesus' return, they became fallen Babylon. God must call His true people out of them.

In her later ministry, however, she took a more positive attitude toward other churches. She spoke of their ministers as "shepherds of the flock,"[80] "teachers of the gospel whose minds have not been called to the special

THE DELAY OF CHRIST'S COMING

truths for this time,"[81] and urged Adventist ministers to come close to them and pray for and with them.[82] When she died in 1915, her 700-book library contained more than 500 by non-Adventist Christian authors.[83] It seems likely that if she had commented on her contemporaries, Hudson Taylor, David Livingstone, George Müller, or Hannah Whitall Smith, her evaluation would have been positive. It is clear that her view of other churches was not entirely negative.

We Adventists face two dangers in our conviction that our church is a fulfillment of prophecy, the bearer of God's final message to the world. On one hand lies the danger of pride, of saying, "I am holier than thou," in which we reason that membership in the true church guarantees our salvation at the coming of Christ. When that happens, faith in the church replaces faith in Christ. This was the error of some Jewish leaders in the days of Christ, who reasoned that because they were children of Abraham they were sure of salvation.

The opposite danger is guilt. If Christ is waiting for us to finish His work, and He has not come, then we must continually weep and mourn for our failures until He does. We become the fulcrum of world history, and we are to blame, at least indirectly, for its continuing tragedies. This would be a heavy burden, and we wonder whether Ellen White really intended us to bear it. Logically, it makes us unattractive to prospective members. Why should they join a church that sadly admits that its failures are the reason the Lord has not come?

Such guilt has often been a convenient scourge in the hands of the would-be reformer. It doesn't matter what his concern is, whether short skirts, long hair, women's ordination, or divorce—he can always argue that he must be right, simply because the Lord hasn't come. If we overemphasize our responsibility for postponing the coming of Christ, we have no defense against this kind of legalism.

Of the two dangers, Ellen White certainly did not stray into the one of pride. The Laodicean criticism of the True Witness (Revelation 3:14-22) prevented that. Her standard of holiness was too high for her to say, "I am holier than thou." She gave no guarantees that the Seventh-day Adventist Church as such was automatically sure of salvation. The nearest she came to such a thing appears in her statements on the future success of the church,[84] but here she refers to the Christian church as a whole. "Church" includes more than "Adventists." She saw the analogy between ancient and modern Israel, and knew that past election does not assure future perseverance. Only he who endures to the end will be saved.

Concerning the factor of guilt, it was indeed one of her emphases after 1883, but we must not stress it more than she did. She believed in God's sovereignty as well as man's responsibility. We must remember that the work is *God's*, and *He* will finish it and cut it short in righteousness. We must see her thought that the Lord is *waiting* for the church to finish proclaiming the three angels' messages along with her parallel teaching that the church must proclaim the message *because* the Lord is coming soon. Only in this way can we recognize her own balance.

FOOTNOTES

[1] "Dear Brethren and Sisters," *Present Truth*, September 1849, p. 31.
[2] *Spiritual Gifts*, vol. 1, p. 148 (in *Early Writings*, p. 243).
[3] James White, "Watchman, What of the Night?" *Review and Herald*, Oct. 9, 1856, p. 184; "The Seven Churches," *Review and Herald*, Oct. 16, 1856, p. 189.
[4] *Testimonies*, vol. 1, pp. 141-146, 179-184, and 185-195. The exhortations Mrs. White mentioned in the latter article were to overcome selfishness, pride, and evil passions, avoid the immodest dress fashions of the world (small bonnets and hoops) and be noblehearted and generous. There is also a section on the new plan of "Systematic benevolence" for supporting the ministers.
[5] *Ibid.*, pp. 186, 187.
[6] "Statistical Report," *SDA Encyclopedia*, p. 1423.

THE DELAY OF CHRIST'S COMING

[7] *Testimonies*, vol. 2, pp. 183-196.
[8] Manuscript 5, 1876.
[9] "Walking in the Light," *Review and Herald*, Oct. 25, 1881, p. 258. James died on August 6.
[10] *Christ's Object Lessons*, pp. 408, 411.
[11] *The Great Controversy*, pp. 393-398, 400, 402, 426-428.
[12] Using the felicitous metaphor of Robert Johnston, "Parabolic Interpretations Attributed to the Tannaim" (Ph.D. diss., Hartford Seminary Foundation, June 1977), pp. 639, 640.
[13] "Preparation for Christ's Coming," *Testimonies* (1879), vol. 4, pp. 306, 307.
[14] "To Those Who Are Receiving the Seal of the Living God," broadside, Jan. 31, 1849 (in *Early Writings*, p. 58).
[15] "The Kingdom and the Church," *Second Coming of Christ*, compiled and edited by Nathaniel West, p. 201.
[16] *Testimonies*, vol. 1, p. 48-52.
[17] *Patriarchs and Prophets*, p. 170.
[18] *The Acts of the Apostles*, p. 536.
[19] *The Desire of Ages*, pp. 31, 32.
[20] *Early Writings*, p. 22; *Testimonies*, vol. 1, p. 72.
[21] "The Review and Herald," *Review and Herald*, Jan. 5, 1869, p. 11.
[22] "Preparation for Christ's Coming," *Testimonies*, vol. 4, p. 306. The same article, however, added that one who believed in the near coming of Christ would show it by being faithful in the business of everyday life. But in another context she rebuked wealthy farmers who acted as if at His coming the Lord would only require them to present to Him their enriched and improved farms. See *Signs of the Times Extra*, Feb. 8, 1892, p. 2. Again the doctrine of the soon coming of Christ served as a hammer pounding many nails.
[23] "Camp Meeting Address," *Testimonies*, vol. 5, p. 9.
[24] "The Day of the Lord at Hand," *Ibid.*, p. 101.
[25] Manuscript 3, 1867.
[26] "To the Church," *Review and Herald*, June 12, 1855, p. 246.
[27] "A Message for Today," *Review and Herald*, June 18, 1901, p. 387.
[28] *Testimonies to Ministers*, pp. 236-238.
[29] "Necessity of the Oil of Grace," *Review and Herald*, Mar. 17, 1894, pp. 193, 194.
[30] Letter 38, 1888.
[31] Manuscript 4, 1883, which now appears in *Selected Messages*, book 1, pp. 59-73.
[32] *Selected Messages*, book 1, pp. 67-69. These three pages contain Mrs. White's reply to the question of the delay of Christ's coming.
[33] *Comparison of the Early Writings of Mrs. White With Later Publications* (Stanberry, Mo.: Church of God Pub. House, 1911 [1883]), p. 3.
[34] It appeared for the first time in Francis McLellan Wilcox, *The Testimony of Jesus: A Review of the Work and Teachings of Mrs. Ellen Gould White* (Washington, D.C.: Review and Herald Pub. Assn., 1934), pp. 92ff.
[35] *Selected Messages*, book 1, p. 189; "Walking in the Light," *Review and Herald*, Oct. 25, 1881, p. 257; *Selected Messages*, book 2, pp. 113, 114.
[36] Nathaniel West, comp., *Second Coming of Christ*, p. 8.
[37] The difference between the KJV text of 2 Peter 3:12 and the margin hangs on transitive and intransitive meanings of the same Greek word. It can be translated both as "hasten" and "hasten unto." Many modern versions, such as the RSV, take it transitively. Mrs. White quoted the intransitive, "hastening

HOW LONG, O LORD?

unto," in *Early Writings*, p. 108, and *The Acts of the Apostles*, p. 536, and the transitive in *The Desire of Ages*, p. 633.

[38] *Spiritual Gifts*, vol. 4, pp. 21-27; *Spirit of Prophecy*, vol. 4, pp. 287-295.

[39] *Selected Messages*, book 1, pp. 67, 68.

[40] At this point Oscar Cullmann, a modern theologian whose position is very close to Adventists', disagrees. He says that the coming of the kingdom does not depend on man's acceptance of the call. The proclamation of the gospel is a sign but not a condition of the end. We can work joyfully, not to hasten the kingdom, but because we know the kingdom comes from God. See his "Eschatology and Missions in the New Testament," in W. D. Davies and David Daube, eds., *The Background of the New Testament and Its Eschatology* (Cambridge: University Press, 1956), pp. 410-413.

[41] Manuscript 173, 1902 (in *The SDA Bible Commentary*, Ellen G. White Comments, vol. 4, p. 1161).

[42] *General Conference Bulletin*, Feb. 28, 1893, p. 419; *Testimonies*, vol. 9, p. 29; *Review and Herald*, Oct. 31, 1899, p. 697; *Christ's Object Lessons*, p. 69; *Testimonies*, vol. 6, p. 450; *Review and Herald*, Dec. 24, 1903, p. 8; *Review and Herald*, Nov. 24, 1904, p. 16.

[43] *Education*, p. 271; *The Acts of the Apostles*, p. 111.

[44] *Spirit of Prophecy*, vol. 4, pp. 291, 292; *The Great Controversy*, pp. 457, 458.

[45] *Testimonies*, vol. 5, pp. 80, 81, 207-216, 449-467.

[46] "Advancing in Christian Experience," sermon preached Oct. 20, 1888, printed in A. V. Olson, *Through Crisis to Victory* (Washington, D.C.: Review and Herald Pub. Assn., 1966), p. 268.

[47] "The Perils and Privileges of the Last Days," *Review and Herald*, Nov. 22, 1892, reprinted in *Selected Messages*, book 1, p. 363.

[48] *Education*, p. 264. Although this idea was common among conservative leaders of her time, modern eschatologists no longer hold it. B. Klappert, "King," in Colin Brown, ed., *New International Dictionary of New Testament Theology*, (Grand Rapids, Mich.: Zondervan, 1976), vol. 2, p. 385, says that the kingdom cannot be hastened by doing battle with God's enemies (as the Zealots hoped) nor forced in by scrupulous observance of the law (as the Pharisees assumed).

[49] *Testimonies*, vol. 7, pp. 35, 36; "The Time of the End," *Review and Herald*, Nov. 23, 1905, p. 6.

[50] Modern theologians agree. G. C. Berkouwer, *The Return of Christ* (Grand Rapids: Eerdmans, 1972), p. 136, wrote: "The meaning of the present dispensation can only be fruitfully discussed in terms of its relation to mandate and exhortation." Karl Barth, *Church Dogmatics* (Edinburgh: T. and T. Clark, 1961), IV/3/1, pp. 331, 332, says that Christ gives His people time to participate in the harvest not only as spectators but as coworkers.

[51] "Witnesses for God," *Signs of the Times*, Oct. 8, 1902, p. 642; "Why the Lord Waits," *Review and Herald*, July 21, 1896, p. 449.

[52] "The Home Missionary Work," *Testimonies*, vol. 6, p. 438.

[53] *Historical Sketches*, p. 287.

[54] Letter 34, 1906, in *Loma Linda Messages* (Payson, Ariz.: Leaves-of-Autumn Books, Inc.), pp. 154-158. It was a letter of encouragement to Burden after he had led in purchasing the first buildings of what is now Loma Linda University in 1905. She assured him that the Lord would be with them in 1906 "as he was with us in 1841, 1842, 1843, and 1844"—showing her constant orientation to the 1844 movement.

[55] *Testimonies*, vol. 7, pp. 15, 35, 36; vol. 6, pp. 14-22, 29, 440-467.

[56] "A Message for Today," *Review and Herald*, June 18, 1901, p. 387.

[57] *Testimonies*, vol. 6, pp. 14, 15, 21; vol. 7, p. 220.

THE DELAY OF CHRIST'S COMING

[58] Letter 184, 1901.
[59] Merlin L. Neff, *For God and C.M.E.: A Biography of Percy T. Magan* (Mountain View, Calif.: Pacific Press Pub. Assn., 1964), pp. 76-78, 92.
[60] *Testimonies*, vol. 5, pp. 714-718.
[61] *Seventh-day Adventist Yearbook of Statistics for 1889* (Battle Creek, Mich.: Review and Herald, 1889), pp. 67, 73-75.
[62] "Under Which Banner?" *Testimonies to Ministers*, p. 364 (Sept. 24, 1895).
[63] *Testimonies*, vol. 5, p. 80.
[64] *Ibid.*, pp. 214, 216; *Review and Herald*, Oct. 6, 1896, p. 629.
[65] Manuscript 5, 1874.
[66] "Prepare the Way of the Lord," *Review and Herald*, Aug. 2, 1898, p. 485.
[67] *Review and Herald*, May 2, 1912, p. 4 (in *Counsels on Health*, p. 248).
[68] *The Great Controversy*, pp. 613, 614.
[69] *The Acts of the Apostles*, pp. 596-599.
[70] *Christ's Object Lessons*, p. 69.
[71] *The Great Controversy*, pp. 648, 649; *Testimonies*, vol. 5, p. 476.
[72] Statements from 1889 and 1898, reproduced in *The SDA Bible Commentary*, vol. 7, p. 978.
[73] *Patriarchs and Prophets*, p. 165; *Testimonies* (1888), vol. 5, pp. 688-692; Letter to Brother S., Mar. 23, 1893 (in *Testimonies to Ministers*, p. 62).
[74] *Testimonies*, vol. 1, p. 363; vol. 4, p. 489; vol. 5, p. 524.
[75] *The Great Controversy*, p. 28.
[76] *Patriarchs and Prophets*, p. 159; *Christ's Object Lessons*, p. 177; *Testimonies*, vol. 9, pp. 95, 96.
[77] "Our Present Duty and the Coming Crisis," *Review and Herald*, Jan. 11, 1887, p. 17.
[78] "Our Responsibility," *Testimonies*, vol. 8, p. 28.
[79] Published in *Review and Herald*, Mar. 22, 29, and Apr. 5, 1892.
[80] *Testimonies*, vol. 6, p. 78.
[81] *Christ's Object Lessons*, p. 230.
[82] *Review and Herald*, Nov. 25, 1890, p. 721 (in *Evangelism*, pp. 562, 563).
[83] Ronald D. Graybill and Warren H. Johns, "An Inventory of Ellen G. White's Library," and "Books in the E. G. White Library in 1915," Ellen G. White Estate Document File 825.
[84] *Prophets and Kings*, pp. 176, 720, 725, 730-733; *The Desire of Ages*, p. 822; *Testimonies to Ministers*, pp. 20, 21; *Evangelism*, p. 707.

CHAPTER V

The Two Streams Merge

Our study of Ellen White's eschatology began by tracing its roots back through William Miller to the Puritans of the seventeenth century. Her conviction that Christ was coming soon was not at all unique. Many before her, basing their faith on the time prophecies of the Bible, had lived and died in the blessed hope.

The time prophecies that men have seen as pointing to the coming of Christ, however, have produced disappointment as often as hope. When Christ did not appear in 1844, the experience destroyed faith in some Millerites and produced fanaticism in others, while a tiny remnant held on to their belief in Jesus' soon coming while admitting they did not know the date. Ellen Harmon [White] belonged to this group, retaining her faith in Miller's calculations because of the cogency of his arguments and because of the spiritual revival she had enjoyed in that belief. She always looked back nostalgically to that glorious expectation and took the dedication of those believers as a model for herself and her readers throughout her ministry.

To explain the disappointment, our spiritual fathers divided Miller's judgment into investigative and executive phases. When Christ finishes the investigative work that He began in 1844, then He will return to save His people and execute judgment on the wicked.

Ellen White and her friends believed that Miller's proclamation fulfilled God's plan even though he did not fully understand his own message. They held that the

THE TWO STREAMS MERGE

Millerite movement itself fulfilled the prophecy of the first angel in Revelation 14:6, 7, and the opposition they experienced from the other churches fulfilled the second angel's message of Revelation 14:8. When they discovered the seventh-day Sabbath and saw the future Sabbath-Sunday conflict in the third angel's message of Revelation 14:9-12, they had a complete system of beliefs that explained their past and gave them a crucial part to play in God's final plans. The three angels' messages commissioned them and us to prepare a people to meet the Lord.

The new body of beliefs gathered out of the tattered and discouraged remnant of the Millerites a dynamic church that in the fourteen decades since has far surpassed its parent in size and international extent. It has retained the inspiration of Miller's expectation, while avoiding date-setting.

We have seen that Ellen White's belief in the nearness of Christ's coming had its basis in time prophecies already completed. Because they were past, the Lord's coming could not be far distant, but because there were none to follow, we could not date it. She knew the last days began in 1798, but she did not know when they would end. Nevertheless the time prophecies remained fundamental to her eschatology, taking priority even ahead of the signs of the time. She always tied the signs to the time prophecies. They took on the quality of signs because they occurred in the end-time.

The prophecies pointing to the return from Babylonian exile and the first advent of Christ provided her with strong support for her confidence in the sovereignty of God. Commenting on them she wrote, "God's purposes know no haste and no delay."[1] If the first advent of Christ depended on the sovereignty of God, the second must be equally so.

Other eschatologists in our time have noticed that the

HOW LONG, O LORD?

New Testament writers saw themselves living already in the last day. For these scholars the problem has been the nineteen centuries since then. How could the last days last so long? It was not a problem for Ellen White, however. She spoke only of a delay since 1844. She emphasized the "time of the end" predictions of Daniel more than the "last days" convictions of John and Paul.

We cannot look at the time element in her eschatology, however, without noticing that she never spoke of the nearness of Christ's coming as a mere point of information. She used it rather as a means to an end, a motive for holy living and diligent witnessing. Her apocalyptic expectations impelled her prophetic exhortations. The nearness of Christ's return became an ethical rather than a chronological statement, as when she wrote that believers should always live in the spirit of Christ's soon advent, and that some erred in not keeping it near enough.

In her early years Mrs. White expected to live until the end. After 1888 we find few such statements, although she continued to speak of the end being near. But the effects of the two emphases were the same. In both she counseled her readers to "live and act wholly in reference to the coming of the Son of man."[2] The stress on "nearness" has the advantage that it can be maintained indefinitely. The expectation of living until the end displayed the enthusiasm of the 100-yard dash. Nearness is the stance for the marathon.

Her program for the church seems to have been influenced by the holiness movement but motivated by the Millerite movement. She saw every true reform as part of the third angel's message. Although she never agreed with the postmillennialists that man can set up the kingdom of God on earth, she did believe that improvements in health, education, temperance, family life, dress, recreation, and giving helped to prepare a people to meet Christ.

THE TWO STREAMS MERGE

Such good deeds, however, are not different from the duties of Christians in all ages. Every believer has always been told to show his faith by his works. The conviction of Christ's soon coming simply lent new urgency to familiar exhortations for Ellen White just as it had for William Miller and the Puritans. She sought to maintain the dedication and drive of the dash throughout the marathon.

The race was long, however, and we ask whether she suffered a "crisis of delay." In the first half of her ministry she spoke at least six times of Christ coming during the lifetime of people then alive—she took the nearness seriously. Did her faith change as years lengthened into decades and the Lord did not appear?

The answer is both yes and no. Yes, because in 1883 she began to say that the Lord's return had indeed been delayed.[3] No, because she knew the reason for the tarrying and at the same time continued to speak of nearness. It was at this time that "delay" joined the "nearness" statements in her writings.

After acknowledging a delay in her 1883 statement, Mrs. White explained it by saying it depended on the state of the church. The Lord could not come because, first, the church was not ready for Him, and second, the gospel had not been preached to the world. In other words, the obligations that she urged on the church because of nearness now became the reason for the delay. The constants in both were the twin duties of holy living and diligent witnessing, rooted in the three angels' messages. A true holiness prophet, Ellen White was deeply burdened over sins in the church. She believed that while Christ was cleansing the sanctuary in heaven He was also doing the same to His people on earth. Christians have always been under obligation to live holy lives, but the conviction that Christ is waiting for His image to be reflected in His children lent new urgency to her call to righteous living.

The second reason Ellen White cited for the delay was the need to fulfill Matthew 24:14. In the language of the first angel, every nation, tribe, tongue, and people must hear the announcement of Jesus' coming before He can return. Other expositors saw it as a sign of the end, but Mrs. White regarded it as a condition to be fulfilled. Ten years before she died, she admitted she had expected Christ to arrive before then but explained that the vision of a *world* to warn had come to her in later years.[4]

This concept of the contingency of Christ's coming served as a powerful reinforcement of her exhortations. It grew logically out of the three angels' messages, which gave the Seventh-day Adventist Church its mission. Only when the church has developed the holiness and preached the message predicted in Revelation 14:6-12 can Jesus return.

When we compare Mrs. White's emphases with those of the Bible, we find statements of both nearness and delay there also. Matthew 24:14 can be taken as a requirement to be fulfilled before Jesus comes. Second Peter 3:8, 9 intimates that the Lord waits because He is not willing that anyone should perish. Matthew 25:1-5 pictures the bridegroom as being delayed, and verses 14-30 show the householder coming back after a long time.

On the other hand, the books of Daniel and Revelation emphasize the sovereignty of God, laying out a sequence of world history under God's control that unfolds in majestic cycles, climaxing at the second advent of Christ. Here, indeed, is the basis of her conviction that the Lord is coming soon. Contingency is not prominent in the prophetic books.

As we read Mrs. White's concept of delay, however, we find that here, as in her statements on nearness, the question of "When?" recedes behind her constant evan-

THE TWO STREAMS MERGE

gelistic appeals. Because they are open-ended, they give no handle to date-setters. No one can predict when the church will be holy enough or the gospel preached widely enough that the Lord can arrive.

We find, then, both harmony and tension in her eschatology, and it is good that it should be so. There is harmony in the apocalyptic roots and the ethical fruits of her two streams of thought. Both originate in the three angels' messages: nearness in the time prophecies ending in 1844, and delay in the obligation to preach the messages to the world. For her the three angels were a commission to service more than a prediction of the future.

The tension in her eschatology appears when we hear her speaking of an appointed time for the return of Christ and also saying He is delayed by the failures of the church. We see it again when she writes of the First Advent that "God's purposes know no haste and no delay,"[5] but of the Second that "the promises and threatenings of God are alike conditional."[6] Both aspects are necessary, however. If we emphasize either without the other, it has bad effects in Christian faith and life. If we stress the nearness only, for instance, and men say that their activities do not hasten or delay Christ's coming, the result is passivity. Why should men be concerned if their actions have no effect on God's plans? But if we speak only of delay, the result is despair. Since the generation of the apostles was not holy enough to meet the standard (for Christ did not return in their time), then what assurance do we have that He will ever come?

Like the Bible itself, Mrs. White retains both sides of the tension, and so should we. She combines God's sovereignty with man's freedom. God Himself knows the time when Jesus will return, but he has been delayed by our failures. It seems like a postponement to us, but she said in 1888 that the apparent tarrying is not so in reality.[7]

HOW LONG, O LORD?

One statement balances another, and we must listen to all of them.

Scholars who say that history has always overwhelmed apocalyptic and that failed expectations show that Christ will not come at all are not being fair to the Bible. In the New Testament itself we find no "crisis of delay," although most of it was written a generation after Jesus said, "This generation shall not pass, till all these things be fulfilled" (Matt. 24:34; Mark 13:30; Luke 21:32). The book of Revelation appeared even later, and it too holds a near expectation without apology. Second Peter 3:8, 9 gave a clear answer to those who denied the reality of Christ's coming altogether and at the same time supplied a reason for the apparent delay in the mercy of God, but it reveals nothing that we could call a crisis of delay.

Skeptics scoff at the Montanists, Puritans, Pietists, and Millerites, who all expected Jesus to return in their time, but all of them found the promise blessed even though they died without seeing it realized. To say that they were all wrong is too shallow an evaluation of their faith. Paul Althaus, well-known theologian of the first half of this century, showed much greater insight when he wrote that all serious and living eschatology has held an imminent expectation of the end and seen the signs in its own time.[8]

Perhaps we can illustrate the nature of eschatological faith with another analogy. A mountain climber often mistakes a lower peak for the top of the mountain simply because he cannot see beyond the lower peak, but he does not give up the climb or deny that the mountain is there. He knows the top certainly lies ahead. In the same way, so far, every date set for the return of Christ has passed, but the spiritual climber does not abandon his faith, for he knows that while lower peaks may obscure the goal, it is surely there. One who is not climbing at all has no hope of

THE TWO STREAMS MERGE

reaching the top. Only he who endures to the end will be saved.

To those who asked when the Lord would come, Ellen White always answered that the end was near but the time unknown. In 1894 she wrote that she had no special light as to when probation would close, but added that it was time to work while the day lasted.[9] Her emphasis was always on the work, not the time. The believer must continually show by his life that he believes that Christ is coming soon.

To those who later inquired as to why the Lord had not come, she replied that He was hindered by the unbelief and disobedience of the church. Her answers to the "When?" and the "Why not yet?" focused on both the obligations of holy living and earnest witnessing. The coming of Christ could be hastened or delayed by the lives and deeds of His people. The exhortations harmonize the nearness and delay statements in her writings.

Ellen White's eschatology is a notable representative of nineteenth-century premillennial expectations. She retained William Miller's expectation by dividing his 1844 judgment into two phases. Her place between the two inspired the "Adventist" portion of Seventh-day Adventist belief, allowing her to keep the Advent near without setting new dates. This position also gave the church its prophetic mission, summarized in the three angels' messages of Revelation 14:6-12, and opened the possibility of delay. Her exhortations were always urgent but never anxious. Because she saw the angels carrying one gospel to all men alike, she did not accept John Nelson Darby's dividing of the world into Israel, church, and Gentile sections, with its splitting of Jesus' coming into a secret rapture for Christians and a public return for Jews. Because she saw future events as constantly impending, she avoided the irrelevance of giving bare facts or making charts. She spoke of tomorrow only to throw light on today. The abiding value of her eschatology lies in its moral appeals to our present dedication and service.

FOOTNOTES

[1] *The Desire of Ages*, p. 32.
[2] *Early Writings*, p. 58.
[3] Manuscript 4, 1883 (in *Selected Messages*, book 1, pp. 66-69).
[4] Letter 34, 1906; see *Loma Linda Messages*, pp. 154-158.
[5] *The Desire of Ages*, p. 32.
[6] *Selected Messages*, book 1, p. 67.
[7] Letter 38, 1888.
[8] "Eschatology," in Jaroslav Pelikan, ed., *Twentieth Century Theology in the Making* (New York: Harper and Row, 1969), vol. 1, p. 289.
[9] "Consequences of Adam's Sin a Warning to Men," *Review and Herald*, Oct. 9, 1894, pp. 625, 626.

CHAPTER VI

How Then Should We Live? The Bible Answer

Ellen White stressed preparation more than time, and so does the Bible. We have noticed that when the disciples asked Jesus whether He would "at this time restore again the kingdom to Israel," He told them that the times and seasons were in the Father's hands, but they were to be His witnesses (Acts 1:6-8). The time of the restoration was not their business—witnessing was. We need to remember His emphasis.

Matthew 24 and its parallels in Mark 13 and Luke 21 give the clearest description of the signs of the end. Mrs. White wrote a verse-by-verse study of these chapters in "On the Mount of Olives" in *The Desire of Ages*.[1] After tracing the destruction of Jerusalem and the persecutions of the Middle Ages, she mentioned the final signs in the heavens and warned against false christs and false prophets. Then she turned to her exhortations and ended with the verse, "Watch ye therefore, and pray always, that ye may be accounted worthy to escape all these things that shall come to pass, and to stand before the Son of man."[2]

How then shall we watch? How should we take heed to ourselves, so that day will not come upon us unawares? How should a Christian live who believes these chapters?

Some today prepare for the end by laying in stocks of food for the time of trouble. Young couples decide not to have children because the end is near. Others drop out of college, feeling the time has come to go home and preach

HOW LONG, O LORD?

the message to their neighbors. They are convinced that the nearness of the end calls them to a new lifestyle.

Christ, however, did not command us to make physical preparations for His coming, nor did He prescribe a different lifestyle for the last generation. Those who stow away food or avoid having children or drop out of school have no command from Him for such actions. The preparation He calls for is quite different.

The answer to the question of Matthew 24 appears in Matthew 25. We should not separate the two chapters. The three parables of chapter 25—the 10 virgins, the talents, and the sheep and goats-teach us how to prepare for the return of Christ.

A number of interesting similarities exist between the three parables. Each depicts two classes of people. In the parable of the virgins, we see the wise and foolish; while in the parable of the talents, we encounter those who improve their talents and those who do not. The sheep and the goats represent those who are kind to others and those who are not.

Another parallel is that each parable points to the great reckoning day, and in each case Jesus brings joy to one class and destruction to the other. Christ is the heavenly bridegroom who welcomes the wise virgins to His wedding banquet. He is the householder who gives the talents and later comes back with a "Well done" for the faithful servants. Finally He is the king who invites those on His right hand to inherit the kingdom of their Father. Still another similarity is the fact that the time of Christ's return is unknown and unexpected in all three parables.

What kind of preparation, then, do the three parables call us to? The parable of the virgins deals with our personal relationship to God—the oil represents the Holy Spirit. All during the waiting time we must make sure we have extra oil in our bottles, lest our lamps go out before the Bridegroom appears. The two groups looked alike until they woke up—only then did the difference emerge, when it was too late to supply their lack. The foolish virgins counted on time they did not have. No preparation was possible at midnight.

Their experience is often repeated. Many young men who never took their faith seriously in academy or college have been caught short when they went into military service. In some countries threatened loss of jobs or lives has revealed who had extra oil with their lamps. Some such test will come to every professed believer. Nearly always it appears suddenly and unexpectedly. There can be no last-minute preparation.

The reward for the wise is a place at the wedding banquet of the Lamb. The loss of the foolish is to be shut out with the tragic words "I don't know you." If we want Him to know us then, we must know Him now!

The parable of the talents tells us how to deal with God's property. We are His stewards during the waiting time. Either we use His talents or lose them. Using them, we multiply them. God expects an increase on His property.

Both parables imply a delay in Christ's return. The bridegroom came while the virgins slept. The householder returned "after a long time." The way to be ready is to be busy improving His goods. In both parables, no frantic last-minute preparations are possible. Only a constant dedication to the Lord's work earns the "Well done" at last.

What are the talents? Ellen White lists abilities common to many. She mentions mental faculties, speech, influence, time (everyone has an equal amount of this), health (which improves with care), strength, money, and kindly impulses.[3] To them we might add cooking, counseling, teaching, preaching, and letterwriting. Any natural ability can be a talent when we improve it for God.

No one has no talents. In the parable, the one with the

least had one. Thus, no one could object that he could do nothing because he had nothing. The one-talent servant should have returned just as high a percentage of increase as the five-talent man. He also could have heard the "Well done."

The reward for the faithful servants was to enter the joy of their Lord, the joy of serving others. There can be no higher joy than this. The reward of the one-talent man in his niggardly selfishness, of course, was that he found no joy and lost what he had.

The parable of the sheep and the goats deals with our relationship to others, to the poor and oppressed. In all three parables those who lose their place with the Lord get shut out not for what they do, but for what they do not do.

The third parable summons us to serve the Lord by serving His other children. It is the parable of unknown goodness and unconscious wickedness. The sheep do not know they are working for Christ. They do good not to serve Him, but simply because they see someone who needs help, and they want to do it. Their response comes from their hearts. Being told they are doing it for Christ is an astonishing surprise.

The goats do not know they are ignoring Christ. They imply that if they had, they would have served Him, but the poor were not worth their attention. Showing no loving-kindness themselves, they receive none from the Lord. Knowing good and not doing it is sin. They do not reap what they have not sowed.

A popular cliché of the current generation is that we ought to have a "relationship with Jesus." Like all clichés, it is losing its value through overuse. Many people suppose it refers to some mystical experience during prayer. Often they set it over against the routines of everyday life. But these parables reveal what our relationship with Jesus should be precisely *in* our everyday lives.

The parable of the virgins tells us we should cultivate

HOW THEN SHOULD WE LIVE? THE BIBLE ANSWER

our devotional lives and keep our vessels full of oil every day. We never know when we may find ourselves thrown into a situation in which we won't have time to study and pray before making a decision or giving an answer.

The parable of the talents teaches us to be diligent about our work, improving every ability the Lord has given us. That may mean going to college, raising children, managing a farm, or preaching a sermon. If the Lord comes and finds us improving our talents, we shall be ready.

The parable of the sheep and goats reminds us to employ our gifts for others. Whatever I have that I can use to help them makes me a debtor to Christ. When I relate to the poor and oppressed, I am relating to Him—this is what it means to have a "relationship with Jesus."

In Matthew 24 and 25, then, we find the same emphasis as in Mrs. White's writings. The question of "When?" in chapter 24 merges into the question of "How should we live?" in chapter 25. It is not for us to know the times and the seasons. The Father has kept these in His own hand. The time of Jesus' coming is one of the secret things that belong only to Him. But our duty during the waiting time is clear. Last-minute preparations are impossible. It is a constant lifestyle of holiness and witness that will receive the kingdom at last.

FOOTNOTES

[1] Pages 627-636.
[2] Page 636.
[3] *Christ's Object Lessons*, pp. 325-365.

APPENDIX

**Ellen G. White Manuscript Release 816
(arranged in chronological order, with titles
supplied by the trustees of the
Ellen G. White Estate)**

1867. *Danger of Not Bringing the Lord's Coming as Near as One Should.* I saw that for some time past, Sister J has had a rebellious spirit, has been self-willed; that her will had not yet been broken; that that will was her idol, and that that idol would shut her out of heaven unless speedily sacrificed. I saw that she did not bring the coming of the Lord as near as she should, and that her mind, instead of being at Rochester [New York], should be all swallowed up in the work of God, and she should be seeking labor wherever there was an opportunity.—Manuscript 3, 1867, p. 1. (To a prominent worker and his wife, c. 1867.)

1875. *How Early Advent Believers Reacted to the Delay in Christ's Coming.* The light is shining forth upon the fourth commandment; God is opening the understanding of many to see that they have been breaking the Lord's Sabbath. "And the temple of God was opened in heaven, and there was seen in his temple the ark of his testament" (Revelation 11:19), calling, as it were, the attention of the people to the law of God covered by the mercy seat; and the angels are represented as all looking reverentially into

APPENDIX

that law. God has made us the repositories of His law. What a responsibility is ours to form characters in harmony with the law of God! We are drawing nearer and still nearer the solemn event of our Lord's appearing, "and every man that hath this hope in him purifieth himself, even as he is pure" (1 John 3:3).

There has been a spirit of freedom in the meetings: the testimonies borne seemed to be spirited and had the right ring. Precious gifts have been entrusted to men. We may improve or abuse them. If we will wisely improve them, we may make those within the sphere of our influence better and we will be enriching ourselves with moral power to be a light to others who are in darkness. . . .

This is the scene of your father's [James White's] earlier labors. Quite a number refer to that time when they first heard the message of Christ's near coming from his lips. They were deeply interested, although they were but children. The impression has never left them, for they were then convicted and their hearts imbued by the Spirit of God which accompanied the message.

Now they are in middle age and understand more fully the doctrine and have a more firm and rich experience in present truth. They speak of their hopes and faith with animated countenance, looking forward and hastening unto the coming of the Son of man in the clouds of heaven with power and great glory. The message of the third angel sounding in solemn warning calls their minds to the sacred truths which once affected their hearts so sensibly. The Lord is good. He is very precious to His people.—Letter 31, 1875, pp. 3, 4. (Written from Richmond, Maine, to W. C. White, Sept. 3, 1875.)

1876. *Coming Delayed to Allow a Larger Span for Repentance*. Who will say God will not do what He says He will do? "Let God be true, but every man a liar" (Rom. 3:4). The Lord is coming in flaming fire to take vengeance on those sinners who know not God and obey not His gospel. And because, in His infinite mercy, He delays His coming to give the world a larger span for repentance, sinners flatter themselves [that] He will never come.

In the public press, in the haunts of sin, as well as in the schools of science so-called, there is one sentiment: They curl the lips with scorn and jest and ridicule at the warnings given them, and look upon the thousands who will not believe. Jests are uttered, witty paragraphs published at the expense of those who wait and look for His appearing, and with fear, like Noah, prepare for the event. This is not new, but as old as sin. It is as false as the father of lies.

When ministers, farmers, merchants, lawyers, great men, and professedly good men shall cry, Peace and safety, sudden destruction cometh. Luke reports the words of Christ, that the day of God comes as a snare—the figure of an animal prowling in the woods for prey and lo, suddenly he is entrapped in the concealed snare of the fowler.—Manuscript 5, 1876, p. 5. ("The Days of Noah," c. 1876.)

1886. *Delay of Christ's Coming Will Seem Short in Eternity.* Dear Brethren and Sisters, Christ is soon to come. Will He find you ready and waiting? The bridal lamps must be kept trimmed and burning. His chariot wheels have been delayed because of His long-suffering to usward, not willing that any should perish, but that all should come to repentance and have eternal life. When we shall stand with the redeemed upon the sea of glass, with harps of God and crowns of glory, and before us the unmeasured eternity, we shall then see how short was the waiting period of probation. "Blessed are those servants, whom the Lord when he cometh shall find watching" (Luke 12:37).—Letter 21, 1886, p. 5. (To Brethren and

APPENDIX

Sisters in Healdsburg, July 9, 1886.)

1886. *Investigative Judgment for the Living Soon to Begin.* I address you who shall have this epistle brought before you, who are leaders, who may be termed princes among the people: "Be ye clean, that bear the vessels of the Lord" (Isa. 52:11). Humble your souls before God. Jesus is in the sanctuary. We are in the great day of atonement, and if the investigative judgment has not already commenced for the living, it will soon begin and to how many are the words of the true witness applicable: "I know thy works, that thou hast a name that thou livest, and art dead. Be watchful, and strengthen the things which remain, that are ready to die: for I have not found thy works perfect before God. Remember therefore how thou hast received and heard, and hold fast, and repent. If therefore thou shalt not watch, I will come on thee as a thief, and thou shalt not know what hour I will come upon thee" (Rev. 3:1-3).

The cases of all will be brought up in the judgment, and if their sins are not confessed, their names will then be blotted from the book of life, and their lot will be with the adulterers and the fornicators, and deceivers, and those who love and make a lie. "Thou hast a few names even in Sardis which have not defiled their garments; and they shall walk with me in white: for they are worthy. He that overcometh, the same shall be clothed in white raiment; and I will not blot out his name out of the book of life, but I will confess his name before my Father, and before his angels" (verses 4, 5).—Letter 51, 1886, p. 11. (To G. I. Butler, Sept. 6, 1886.)

1886. *Though Anxious for Heaven, Ellen White Not in a Hurry.* I am much blessed of the Lord, although very much burdened, and I love Jesus with my whole affections. I think our warfare must be nearly ended. I think we are nearing home. I am rejoiced to think the rest will soon come, but even here in this hope I am not in a hurry.

I want to do all my work with patience and fidelity day by day. There are many souls to be saved, and we will be glad that the coming of the Lord is delayed to give them a little more opportunity to get ready. But once saved in the kingdom of God—only think of it—once beyond the temptations and warfare of this life, once in the haven of rest, in the presence of our adorable Redeemer—what will it be!

These light afflictions, Paul says, which are but for a moment, work "for us a far more exceeding and eternal weight of glory; while we look not at the things which are seen, but at the things which are not seen" (2 Cor. 4:17, 18). God help us to look at the brightness of our Saviour's countenance, and clouds will be dispelled. We must have more faith.—Letter 84, 1886, pp. 12, 13. (To G. I. Butler and S. N. Haskell, Sept. 14, 1886.)

1888. *1844 Date Not Revealed in Vision Before the Disappointment.* It was this oft-repeated charge of suppression that led us to determine to gather up all my earliest publications and republish in the book called *Early Writings*, by Mrs. E. G. White. We printed this little book to be scattered everywhere that all might, if they chose, become acquainted with facts. But this did not—only for a time—quiet their reports. They came again just as fresh as though that book had never been printed.

I was a firm believer in definite time in 1844, but this prophetic time was not shown me in vision, for it was some months *after* the passing of this period of time before the first vision was given me. There were many proclaiming a new time after this, but I was shown that we should not have another definite time to proclaim to the people. All who are acquainted with me and my work will testify

APPENDIX

that I have borne but one testimony in regard to the setting of the time.

I have been shown that our disappointment in 1844 was not because of failure in the reckoning of prophetic periods, but in the events to take place. The earth was believed to be the sanctuary. But the sanctuary which was to be cleansed at the end of the prophetic periods was the heavenly sanctuary and not the earth as we all supposed. The Saviour did enter the Most Holy Place in 1844 to cleanse the sanctuary, and the investigative judgment had commenced for the dead. I have been repeatedly urged to accept the different periods of time proclaimed for the Lord to come.

I have ever had one testimony to bear: The Lord will not come at that period, and you are weakening the faith of even Adventists, and fastening the world in their unbelief. There have been plainly set before me events of great and thrilling interest, which must transpire before Christ will come. Satan will move mightily from beneath and will delude the world, while the Lord God Omnipotent will move from above and prepare a people to stand in the great day of His wrath.

The time-setters have pronounced the curse of the Lord upon me as an unbeliever who said, My Lord delayeth His coming. But I have told them that the books of heaven would not make my record thus, for the Lord knows that I loved and longed for the appearing of Christ. But their oft-repeated message of definite time was exactly what the enemy wanted, and it served his purpose well to unsettle the faith in the first proclamation of time, which was of heavenly origin.

The world placed all time-proclamation on the same level and called it a delusion, fanaticism, and heresy. Ever since 1844 I have borne my testimony that we were now in a period of time in which we are to take heed to ourselves lest our hearts be overcharged with surfeiting and drunk-

HOW LONG, O LORD?

enness, and cares of this life, and so that day come upon us unawares. Our position has been one of waiting and watching, with no time-proclamation to intervene between the close of the prophetic periods in 1844 and the time of our Lord's coming. We do not know the day nor the hour, or when the definite time is, and yet the prophetic reckoning shows us that Christ is at the door.

We have not cast away our confidence, neither have we a message dependent upon definite time, but we are waiting and watching unto prayer, looking for and loving the appearing of our Saviour, and doing all in our power for the preparation of our fellowmen for that great event. We are not impatient. If the vision tarry, wait for it, for it will surely come, it will not tarry. Although disappointed, our faith has not failed, and we have not drawn back to perdition. The apparent tarrying is not so in reality, for at the appointed time our Lord will come, and we will, if faithful, exclaim, "Lo, this is our God; we have waited for him, and he will save us" (Isa. 25:9).

I have also been pronounced a deceiver because I have said, "The Lord will soon come; get ready, get ready that we may be found waiting, watching and loving His appearing." But in the Revelation I read this statement, "Behold, I come quickly; and my reward is with me, to give every man according as his work shall be" (Rev. 22:12). "Behold, I come quickly: blessed is he that keepeth the sayings of the prophecy of this book" (verse 7). "Behold, I come quickly: hold that fast which thou hast, that no man take thy crown" (Rev. 3:11). Was the One who bore this testimony a deceiver, because the "quickly" has been protracted longer than our finite minds could anticipate? It is the faithful and true witness that speaks. His words are verity and truth.

If I have failed to make this matter plain which you wish to understand, write me again and I will endeavor to make every point plain and clear. But I must plead not

APPENDIX

guilty to the charge of seeing in vision that the Lord would come at a definite day and hour, which has since passed by.—Letter 38, 1888, pp. 3-5. (To Dear Sister, Aug. 11, 1888.)

1890. *Reason for Establishment of SDA Colleges.* What is the object of establishing colleges among Seventh-day Adventists? It is to provide for our youth, so far as possible, the very best instruction—that which is free from error and in every respect pure from corrupting influences. There are in our land schools in abundance where education in the sciences may be carried to a high point, but they fail to reach the Bible standard of education. The fear of the Lord is the beginning of wisdom. The Lord must preside in our institutions of learning, or the object for which they were brought into existence, with great outlay of means, will fail of being accomplished. We profess to believe important truth, that the Lord is soon coming in the clouds of heaven with power and great glory to take the faithful to the higher school in the mansions He has gone to prepare for them. We should meet a standard very much higher than do those who do not believe these solemn truths.—Letter 25a, 1890, pp. 4, 5. (To Brother Graham, July 14, 1890.)

1891. *We Are to Be Ever Ready for Christ's Coming.* We want to understand our proper relation to God: we want to know how we stand in the presence of God. I want you to see that it is not in the providence of God that any finite man shall, by any device or reckoning that he may make of figures, or of symbols, or of types, know with any definiteness in regard to the very period of the Lord's coming. What shall we know? We are to study the signs which show that He is at the door. You may say, "I have expected it, and I have waited a long time, and the Master has not come yet; and this long time of waiting makes me think that He is not coming." Just so those foolish virgins began to think. They did not have any supply of grace to enable them to stand the test or trial.

Yes, it takes time, and God knew it; and He takes time to test us and to prove us, to see who has the real, genuine righteousness of Christ, and He will test us to see if we can bear with patience, waiting and watching, and working as well. We may be waiting, but not in idle expectancy, saying, "I will not plant that tree because the Lord is coming. I will not do this work in building a meetinghouse for the people to assemble to worship God, because the Lord is coming." No: if the Lord is coming, we want to work with the more diligence to uphold and to gather the Lord's sheep and to bring them into the fold. We want our colleges. Why? Because we want to bring the students out of the world that they may leave its practices, its customs, its superstitions, and its policy: and that they may be educated as to what truth is.

It means something to bring practical religion into the life. There are so many who profess godliness, and yet you cannot distinguish by their dress, by their appearance, by their conversation, by their deportment, or by any of their actions, that there is any difference between them and the world.

We are to represent Jesus Christ. We are to look at His character, at His life of self-denial, patience, kindness, and forbearance. He ate with publicans and sinners, not that He might partake of their luxuries, or their amusements, or of their feasting, but that He might diffuse the precious gems of truth, and scatter these gems as He was sitting at their table. And those precious jewels of truth which fell from His lips would remain in their hearts. And although they might not yield at once to the influence of the Spirit of God, they would be affected by them and finally yield to them. Why? Because He is drawing them all the time. — Manuscript 9, 1891, pp. 7, 8. ("Make Proper Use of

APPENDIX

Talents," sermon preached at Battle Creek, Michigan, Aug. 22, 1891.)

1895. *Spending Too Much Time Getting Educated in the United States.* I would counsel you not to advise Pomare [a Maori student from New Zealand sent to Battle Creek to gain a training to work among his people] to remain in Battle Creek longer. Let him go to his field of labor, to use the knowledge that he has already gained, and in yoking up with Jesus Christ he will become a laborer together with God. The loading down of one man with degree after degree of study will not take the place of learning in the school of Christ His meekness and His lowliness of heart. "Learn of me,"' said the greatest Teacher the world ever knew, "for I am meek and lowly in heart: and ye shall find rest unto your souls" (Matt. 11:29).

I was urged to send Sister Houlder to Battle Creek. My purse paid her expenses, for her soul was in peril. Then I have paid, I do not know just how much, for Brother Lacey to go through his studies. Sister Caro has carried Brother Pomare, which has consumed large sums of money. I promised her I would help her bear the burden of expense, not expecting that he was to be kept years in gaining an education to work among his own people. Willie, now in New Zealand, states that he has sent for drafts from London and Battle Creek for sixty pounds to be paid to Sister Caro to relieve her of embarrassment.

Money has been sent to support Brother Lyndon in school. He had a very good education before he went to America, and should have been in his field of labor long since, and at work. In this country it means much to transfer the means so essential to advance the work in fields that have not been entered, and consume this means, of which there is a dearth, in sending students to be educated in any lines to help us in the work here. And then time is passing and money expended, and the work moving so slowly because of the need of energetic workmen to enter the new fields and practice in the service of Christ in giving to perishing souls the light of truth, present, testing truth.

We feel the need of more help, but the conference has no money to pay the expenses of laborers to return to this country or to transport laborers. We know not what to do. I am distressed over the situation. I am now paying these workers $19 per week, and they support their families and give their services. I could do more of this work if I had the money to do it with. This sum was increased until I paid five pounds per week.—Letter 46, 1895, pp. 2, 3. (To J. H. Kellogg, Apr. 15, 1895.)

1897. *Sunday Laws in Australia*. We are having interesting times for all in Australia. The pressure of the Sunday law has come and is coming. It has been ordered that all stores shall be closed on Sunday, and this is being rigidly enforced. The government is trying to have God acknowledged in the constitution. Our people are making just as vigorous a stand as possible that it shall not be. They have been securing names to a petition to this effect. We can see that that which we have been talking about for the last thirty-five years—this law causing the Sunday to be exalted and making human inventions take the place of God's holy day—is now being fulfilled. There is much excitement now in regard to these matters.

The Second Epistle of Paul to the Thessalonians should be read in connection with these things. The same work of oppression and persecution which was suffered by the saints of God in Paul's day is soon to come to all who believe in this age.—Letter 28, 1897, pp. 1, 2. (To Brother and Sister Belden, July 29, 1897.)

1898. *Advent Delayed Because Work Not Done for the Wicked*. As in the days that were before the Flood, the

APPENDIX

impenitent see no cause for alarm. They eat, they drink, they marry and are given in marriage. The event has been long foretold, but time has passed on, and many distinctly say, "My Lord delayeth His coming." It is because the work has not been done for the wicked that time delays.

God's long forbearance is wonderful. The Master is treated with disrespect, He receives but little thanksgiving for His bestowment of blessings. The world is mad. They do not consider that His long forbearance toward the wicked is a part of His great plan, that judgments will surely come. But the long-suffering God will do His work. He will discriminate with justice and accuracy. —Manuscript 151, 1898, p. 6. (Notes of the Queensland camp meeting, copied Nov. 2, 1898.)

1901. *May Have to Remain Here Many More Years*. Your letter from Chicago received yesterday. I am very sorry that circumstances have taken the shape that they have, but why are you so faithless? Thank the Lord that you have few students, because you are not prepared for a large number. Brother Sutherland and yourself have done bravely and well, and why will you worry yourself out of the arms of your precious Saviour? Has the bank of heaven failed? Have you overdrawn the resources? Is Christ, the light of the world, in Joseph's new tomb? Do we not read, "Wherefore he is able also to save them to the uttermost that come unto God by him, seeing he ever liveth to make intercession for them" (Heb. 7:25)? Now look away from every discouraging presentation, because we have a living Christ to save them to the uttermost that come unto God by Him. The bank of heaven has not failed; you have not overdrawn. . . .

Now in regard to the school, you seem to think that the plant is to put forth full bloom, lilies, roses, and pinks before the root is fully set deep to do this grand work. You must begin small, and not think that you can show all strength in establishing a school after an advanced order, taking in higher studies, and do not worry about leading teachers or under teachers before you have sufficient students to warrant the steps you take. Let not human pride hurt your record. Do not you suppose the Lord sees and is acquainted with the favorable and unfavorable presentations? Has not the Lord an oversight over His own work? You may suppose, my brethren, that you have to do all the devising, all the strengthening, and all the organizing, and I ask you, Is it not best to show that you have confidence in God? Is it not best to consider that our God is manager—that He is director? You must not be anxious to develop too fast. The hand of providence is holding the machinery. When that hand starts the wheel, then all things will begin to move.

How can finite man carry the burdens of responsibility for this time? His people have been far behind. Human agencies under the divine planning may recover something of what is lost because the people who had great light did not have corresponding piety, sanctification, and zeal in working out God's specified plans. They have lost to their own disadvantage what they might have gained to the advancement of the truth if they had carried out the plans and will of God. Man cannot possibly stretch over that gulf that has been made by the workers who have not been following the divine Leader.

We may have to remain here in this world because of insubordination many more years, as did the children of Israel, but for Christ's sake, His people should not add sin to sin by charging God with the consequence of their own wrong course of action. Now, have men who claim to believe the Word of God learned their lesson that obedience is better than sacrifice? "He hath showed thee [this rebellious people], O man, what is good; and what doth the Lord require of thee, but to do justly, and to love mercy, and to walk humbly with thy God?" (Micah 6:8).

APPENDIX

Now the Lord will not be pleased with those men whom He hath appointed to do a certain work, to take on many lines of work and carry them until they become so wearisome that it breaks their strength. You, nor any other agency, cannot heal the hurt that has come to God's people by neglect to lift up His standard and occupy new territory. The churches should now be acting in their strength, with capabilities, talents, and means, carrying the work, reaching higher and broader in capacity to stand before the world in the power of invincible truth.

But if all now would only see and confess and repent of their own course of action in departing from the truth of God, and following human devising, then the Lord would pardon. Warnings have been coming, but they have been unheeded. But a few who may now seek to bridge the gulf that stands so offensively before God must make haste slowly, else the standard bearers will fail, and who will take their place?

Now, my brother, I am deeply sorry for you and your family. I reproach thee not for thy zeal, for if others had shared thy burdens as they should have done, the work would have been far advanced. But now, just now, you must come apart and rest awhile. Be not concerned in regard to your wages. God will not leave you without some help and comfort for yourself, your wife, and little ones. Be of good courage in the Lord. Trust Him fully. Let the Lord carry the burden of the school. You are not to become loaded down with burdens that will accomplish only the work that finite man can do. When you put your trust wholly in God, then you will see in every passage of your experience One going before you preparing the way.

I cannot tell you what you should do, but I can tell you what not to do: Do not worry, be not unbelieving, and do not think that you can blossom into a perfect school at its very planting on new soil. You must remember that it takes time to plant, and to perfect that plant. You just hold fast every inch you have.—Letter 184, 1901, pp. 1-6. (To Prof. P. T. Magan during the early months of his endeavor to establish the college at Berrien Springs, Michigan. Written at South Lancaster, Massachusetts, Dec. 7, 1901.)

1902. *Filled With the Spirit of Christ's Second Advent.* We are looking for the second coming of our Lord and Saviour Jesus Christ. We are not only to believe that the end of all things is at hand. We are to be filled with the spirit of Christ's advent, that when the Lord comes, he may find us ready to meet Him, whether we are working in the field, or building a house, or preaching the Word; ready to say, "Lo, this is our God; we have waited for him, and he will save us" (Isa. 25:9). [Released at a different time, this paragraph carries release number 899.]

Our work is to prepare a people for the soon coming of the Lord. We are to be in the world, but not of the world. Let us consider the work before us. Never forget, we are laborers together with God. We are to prepare the way of the Lord. Let us bind ourselves to His sacred work. We have no time to lose in inaction. We must provide facilities for the accomplishment of the missionary work that the Lord has said must be done. We must teach old and young, men and women, to lay up treasure beside the throne of God.—Letter 25, 1902, p. 5. (To those in Responsible Positions in the Southern Field, Feb. 5, 1902.)

1903. *How E. G. White Faced the Future and Christ's Coming.* The Lord is soon to come, and I must be prepared to meet Him in peace. I am sure that the world is ripening for the last great conflict. I am determined to do all in my power to impart light to those around me. I am not to be sad, but cheerful, and I am to keep the Lord Jesus ever before me. He is coming soon, and we must be ready and waiting for His appearing. O how glorious it will be to see Him and be saved through His merits. Long we have

APPENDIX

waited, but our faith is not to become weak. It is to grow stronger as we see the signs of the times fulfilling. The end is near and we are to put all our energies into the work of preparing to move from this lower school to the school above.—Letter 94, 1903, p. 1. (To Lucinda Hall, May 21, 1903.)

BIBLIOGRAPHY

Ellen G. White Materials

Books:

The Acts of the Apostles. Mountain View, Calif.: Pacific Press, 1911.
Christ's Object Lessons. Washington, D.C.: Review and Herald, 1900, 1941.
Comprehensive Index to the Writings of Ellen G. White. Three volumes. Mountain View, Calif.: Ellen G. White Estate, 1962-1963.
Counsels on Health. Mountain View, Calif.: Pacific Press, 1951.
Counsels to Parents, Teachers, and Students. Mountain View, Calif.: Pacific Press, 1913.
Counsels on Stewardship. Washington, D.C.: Review and Herald, 1940.
The Desire of Ages. Mountain View, Calif.: Pacific Press, 1898, 1940.
Early Writings. Washington, D.C.: Review and Herald, 1882, 1945.
Education. Mountain View, Calif.: Pacific Press, 1903, 1952.
Evangelism. Washington, D.C.: Review and Herald, 1946.
Fundamentals of Christian Education. Nashville: Southern Pub. Assn., 1923.
Gospel Workers. Washington, D.C.: Review and Herald, 1915.
The Great Controversy. Mountain View, Calif.: Pacific Press, 1888, 1950.
Life Sketches. Mountain View, Calif.: Pacific Press, 1915.
Loma Linda Messages. Payson, Ariz.: Leaves-of-Autumn Books, n.d.
Maranatha, The Lord Is Coming. Washington, D.C.: Review and Herald, 1976.
Medical Ministry. Mountain View, Calif.: Pacific Press, 1932.
Messages to Young People. Nashville: Southern Pub. Assn., 1930.
The Ministry of Healing. Mountain View, Calif.: Pacific Press, 1905, 1942.
Patriarchs and Prophets. Mountain View, Calif.: Pacific Press, 1890, 1958.
Prophets and Kings. Mountain View, Calif.: Pacific Press, 1917, 1943.
Selected Messages. Washington, D.C.: Review and Herald, 1958, 1980. 3 books.
The Seventh-day Adventist Bible Commentary. Washington, D.C.: Review and Herald, 1957, Vol. 7-A.
Special Testimonies, Series A, No. 1. Battle Creek, Mich.: SDA General Conference, n.d.
Special Testimonies, Series B, No. 13. South Lancaster, Mass.: South Lancaster Printing Co., 1908.
The Spirit of Prophecy. Battle Creek, Mich.: Steam Press of the Seventh-day Adventist Publishing Assn., 1870-1884. 4 vols.
Spiritual Gifts. Battle Creek, Mich.: Steam Press, 1858-1864. 4 vols.
Steps to Christ. New York: Fleming Revell, 1892.
Testimonies for the Church. Mountain View, Calif.: Pacific Press, 1885-1909. 9 vols.
Testimonies to Ministers and Gospel Workers. Mountain View, Calif.: Pacific Press, 1923.

BIBLIOGRAPHY

That I May Know Him. Washington, D.C.: Review and Herald, 1964.
Thoughts From the Mount of Blessing. Mountain View, Calif.: Pacific Press, 1896, 1956.
A Word to the "Little Flock." With Joseph Bates and James W. White. Brunswick, Maine: James White, 1847, facsimile reproduction by the Review and Herald.

Magazine Articles in Chronological Order:
Present Truth:

"Dear Brethren and Sisters." August 1849, p. 21-24; September 1849, pp. 31, 32.

Review and Herald
(which appeared with slight changes of name in the early years):

"Experience and Views." *Extra*, July 21, 1851, p. 16 (reproduced in *Early Writings*, pp. 11-35).
"To the Brethren and Sisters." June 10, 1852, p. 21.
"To the Saints Scattered Abroad." Feb. 17, 1853, p. 155, 156.
"To the Church." June 12, 1855, p. 246.
"The Future." Dec. 31, 1857, p. 59.
"Communication From Sister White; Slavery and the War." Aug. 27, 1861, pp. 100-102.
"The Future." May 27, 1862, p. 202, 203.
"An Extract From a Letter Written to a Distant Female Friend." Sept. 16, 1862, p. 126.
"The Review and Herald." Jan. 5, 1869, pp. 10, 11.
"Remarks by Mrs. E. G. White, at the Tent-Meeting in Oakland, July 2, 1869." Aug. 17, 1869, p. 57.
"Practical Remarks." Mar. 29, 1870, p. 113-115.
"The Laodicean Church." Sept. 16, 1873, p. 109.
"Our Camp-Meetings." July 10, 1879, p. 17.
"Walking in the Light." Oct. 25, 1881, pp. 257, 258.
"The Advent Faith." Nov. 29, 1881, pp. 337, 338.
"Our Present Position." Aug. 28, 1883, pp. 545, 546.
"Notes of Travel." Nov. 13, 1883, pp. 705, 706.
"Notes of Travel." Oct. 28, 1884, pp. 673, 674.
"The Work for Our Time." Oct. 20, 1885, pp. 641, 642.
"A Missionary Appeal." Dec. 15, 1885, pp. 769, 770.
"The Conference in Sweden." Oct. 5, 1886, pp. 609, 610.
"An Appeal." Oct. 12, 1886, pp. 625-627.
"Our Present Duty and the Coming Crisis." Jan. 11, 1887, pp. 17, 18.
"The Church's Great Need." Mar. 22, 1887, pp. 177, 178.
"Cast Not Away Your Confidence." July 31, 1888, pp. 481, 482.
"The Book of Books." Aug. 21, 1888, pp. 529, 530 (also in *Fundamentals of Christian Education*, pp. 129-137).
"The Approaching Crisis." *Extra*, Dec. 11, 1888, pp. 4, 5.
"The Present Crisis." Jan. 1, 1889, pp. 1, 2.
"The Duty of the Present Hour." Apr. 23, 1889, pp. 257, 258.
"God Warns Men of His Coming Judgments." Nov. 5, 1889, pp. 689, 690.

HOW LONG, O LORD?

"An Address in Regard to the Sunday Movement." *Extra,* Dec. 24, 1889, pp. 2, 3.
"Changed Into His Image." Apr. 28, 1891, p. 257.
"It Is Not for You to Know the Times and the Seasons." Mar. 22, pp. 177, 178; Mar. 29, pp. 193, 194; Apr. 5, 1892, pp. 209, 210.
"Christ's Instruction to His Followers." Apr. 26, 1892, pp. 257, 258.
"The Perils and Privileges of the Last Days." Nov. 22, 1892, pp. 722, 723.
"Consequences of Adam's Sin a Warning to Men." Oct. 9, 1894, pp. 625, 626.
"The Great Need of the Holy Spirit." July 23, 1895, pp. 465, 466.
"Why the Lord Waits." July 21, 1896, pp. 449, 450.
"Whosoever Will, Let Him Come." Oct. 6, 1896, pp. 629, 630.
"Pray for the Latter Rain." Mar. 2, 1897, pp. 129, 130.
"The Perils of the Last Days." Mar. 16, 1897, pp. 161, 162.
"The Bible in Our Schools." Aug. 17, 1897, pp. 513, 514.
"What the Revelation Means to Us." Aug. 31, 1897, pp. 545, 546.
"Go, Preach the Gospel." Mar. 15, 22, 1898, pp. 165, 166, 181, 182.
"Waiting and Working for Christ." Apr. 12, 1898, pp. 229, 230.
"'All That Will Live Godly in Christ Jesus Shall Suffer Persecution.'" Apr. 19, 1898, pp. 245, 246.
"'Prepare Ye the Way of the Lord.'" Aug. 2, 1898, pp. 485, 486.
"The First and the Second Advent." Sept. 5, 1899, pp. 565, 566.
"The Parable of the Ten Virgins." Oct. 31, 1899, pp. 697, 698.
"Lessons From the Christ-Life." Oct. 2, 1900, pp. 625, 626.
"Prepare to Meet the Lord." Nov. 27, 1900, pp. 753, 754.
"Labors in California." Feb. 12, 1901, pp. 97, 98.
"Our Duty to Leave Battle Creek." Apr. 14, 1903, pp. 17-19.
"A Worldwide Message." Aug. 20, 1903, pp. 8, 9.
"Carrying Forward the Lord's Work." Dec. 24, 1903, pp. 8, 9.
"The Work in Washington." July 14, 1904, pp. 8, 9.
"The Closing Work." Oct. 13, 1904, p. 7.
"The Day of the Lord Is Near, and Hasteth Greatly." Nov. 24,1904, pp. 16, 17.
"Lessons From the Life of Solomon—No. 9." Nov. 9, 1905, pp. 9, 10.
"The Time of the End." Nov. 23, 1905, pp. 6, 7.
"Individual Consecration Needed." Nov. 23, 1905, pp. 15-17.
"The San Francisco Earthquake." May 24, 1906, pp. 7, 8.
"Notes of Travel—No. 3. The Judgments of God on Our Cities." July 5, 1906, pp. 7-9.
"Drunkenness and Crime." Oct. 25, 1906, pp. 8, 9 (also in *Temperance,* p. 25).
"'Prepare Ye the Way of the Lord.'" Nov. 1, 1906, pp. 7, 8.
"A Solemn Message to the Church." Nov. 8, 1906, p. 8.
"'Even at the Door.'" Nov. 22, 1906, pp. 19, 20.
"The Return of the Exiles—No. 2; The Decree of Cyrus." Mar. 28, 1907, pp. 8, 9.
"Notes of Travel—No. 6; Loma Linda and Los Angeles." Sept. 5, 1907, pp. 8, 9.
"A Message to Our Churches." Jan. 28, 1909, pp. 7, 8.
"Go, Preach the Gospel." Nov. 17, 1910, pp. 6-8.
"A Study of Principles—No. 5; Methods of Labor Where Prejudice Is Strong." Apr. 6, 1911, pp. 5, 6. D. E. Robinson wrote this article, which quotes Mrs.

BIBLIOGRAPHY

White's answer to the question of whether Sabbathkeepers in the South should work on Sunday when the law forbade it. She gave her reply on Nov. 20, 1895, at a special meeting called to consider the question, on the Armadale camp ground in Victoria, Australia.
"Nearness of the End." Mar. 14, 1912, pp. 3, 4.
"Words of Greeting From Sister White" (to the men gathered at the General Conference session). May 29, 1913, p. 515.
"The Blessed Hope." Nov. 13, 1913, pp. 1110, 1111.
"Preparing for Christ's Return." Nov. 12, 1914, pp. 21, 22.
"A Message for Our Young People." Apr. 15, 1915, p. 3.
"The Last 153 Days." July 23, 1970, pp. 2, 3.

Signs of the Times:

"The Faith of Abraham." Apr. 1, 1875, p. 162.
"Mrs. Ellen G. White, Her Life, Christian Experience, and Labors." Jan. 20, p. 60 and Mar. 3, 1876, p. 100.
"Noah's Time and Ours." Jan. 3, 1878, p. 1.
"The Barren Fig Tree." Feb. 21, 1878, p. 57.
"The Christian's Hope." May 29, 1884, p. 321.
"Watchfulness and Prayer." Jan. 7, 1886, p. 1.
"Women as Christian Laborers." Sept. 16, 1886, p. 561.
"The Coming of the Lord." Nov. 10, 1887, pp. 673, 674.
"I Will Come Again." Jan. 27, 1888, pp. 49, 50.
"'Serve the Lord With Gladness.'" Feb. 3, 1888, pp. 65, 66.
"Looking for That Blessed Hope." June 24, 1889, pp. 369, 370.
"The Work of God's People." Oct. 14, 1889, pp. 609, 610.
"The Danger of Skepticism in Our Youth." Apr. 21, 1890, pp. 241, 242.
"Faith and Works." *Extra*, Feb. 8, 1892, p. 2.
"The Necessity of Receiving the Holy Spirit." Aug. 1, 1892, p. 599.
"'They That Have Done Good.'" Aug. 29, 1892, pp. 662, 663.
"The Doom of Sodom a Warning for the Last Days." Oct. 16, 1893, pp. 774, 775.
"Christ Came to Break Sin's Chain." Apr. 16, 1894, p. 372.
"Delusions of the Last Days." May 28, 1894, pp. 450, 451.
"Satanic Delusions to Increase." June 4, 1894, pp. 466, 467.
"What Manner of Persons Ought Ye to Be?" Oct. 1, 1894, pp. 739, 740.
"The Seal of God, No. 2." Nov. 8, 1899, pp. 722, 723.
"The Present Crisis." Nov. 28, 1900, p. 763.
"The Days of the Son of Man." Apr. 17, 1901, pp. 243, 244.
"The Coming Crisis." Oct. 9, 1901, p. 643.
"Witnesses for God." Oct. 8, 1902, p. 642.
"Our Preparation for the End." Nov. 22, 1905, p. 745.

Others:

"To Those Who Are Receiving the Seal of the Living God." Broadside, Jan. 31, 1849.
"Christ Our Life." *Bible Echo and Signs of the Times.* Jan. 15, 1889, p. 1.
General Conference Bulletin. Feb. 28, 1893, pp. 192, 193, 419; May 27, 1913, pp. 164, 165; May 29, 1913, p. 515.

151

HOW LONG, O LORD?

Unpublished Letters and Manuscripts, Located in the Ellen G. White Research Center, Andrews University, Berrien Springs, Michigan (in chronological order)

Manuscript 3, 1867, to a prominent worker and his wife, c. 1867.
Letter 31, 1875, to W. C. White, Sept. 3, 1875.
Manuscript 5, 1876.
Letter 21, 1886, to Brethren and Sisters in Healdsburg. July 9, 1886.
Letter 51, 1886, to G. I. Butler, Sept. 6, 1886.
Letter 84, 1886, to G. I. Butler and S. N. Haskell, Sept. 14, 1886.
Letter 38, 1888, to Dear Sister, Aug. 11, 1888.
Letter 25a, 1890, to Brother Graham, July 14, 1890.
Manuscript 9, 1891, sermon preached at Battle Creek, Mich., Aug. 22, 1891.
Letter 46, 1895, to J. H. Kellogg, Apr. 15, 1895.
Letter 28, 1897, to Brother and Sister Belden, July 29, 1897.
Manuscript 151, 1898, notes of the Queensland camp meeting, copied Nov. 2, 1898.
Letter 184, 1901, to Prof. P. T. Magan, Dec. 7, 1901.
Letter 66, 1901, to Bro. Kilgore, June 26, 1901.
Letter 25, 1902, to Those in Responsible Positions in the Southern Field, Feb. 5, 1902.
Letter 94, 1903, to Lucinda Hall, May 21, 1903.
Letter 34, 1906, to Brother and Sister Burden, Jan. 19, 1906, from Sanitarium, Calif. Reproduced in *Loma Linda Messages*, (Payson, Ariz.: Leaves-of-Autumn reprint), pp. 154-158 (which corresponds to pp. 266-273 of Burden's original collection).

Selected Other Books

Adams, Roy. *The Sanctuary Doctrine, Three Approaches in the Seventh-day Adventist Church*. Andrews University Seminary Doctoral Dissertation series, vol. 1. Berrien Springs, Mich.: Andrews University Press, 1981.

Ahlstrom, Sydney. *A Religious History of the American People*. New Haven, Conn.: Yale University Press, 1972.

Andreasen, Jens-Évald. "A Comparative Study of Phoebe Palmer and Ellen G. White in the Period Before 1850." Term paper, Document File 2122-C, Ellen G. White Research Center, Andrews University, Berrien Springs, Mich., n.d.

Andreasen, M. L. *The Book of Hebrews*. Washington, D.C.: Review and Herald, 1948.

────. *The Sanctuary Service*. 2nd ed., rev. Washington, D.C.: Review and Herald, 1937, 1947; softback ed., 1969.

Ball, Bryan W. *A Great Expectation: Eschatological Thought in English Protestantism to 1660*. Leiden: E. J. Brill, 1975.

Bacchiocchi, Samuele. *Divine Rest for Human Restlessness*. Berrien Springs, Mich.: Dr. Samuele Bacchiocchi, 1980.

Barth, Karl. *Church Dogmatics*. Edinburgh: T. & T. Clark, 1961, 1962.

Bates, Joseph. *Second Advent Way Marks and High Heaps, or a Connected View of the Fulfillment of Prophecy by God's Peculiar People, From the Year 1840 to 1847*. New

BIBLIOGRAPHY

Bedford, Mass.: Benjamin Lindsey, 1847.

_____. *The Seventh Day Sabbath, a Perpetual Sign, From the Beginning to the Entering Into the Gates of the Holy City, According to the Commandment.* 2nd rev., enl. ed. New Bedford, Mass.: by the author, 1847 (1st ed., 1846).

Battistone, Joseph. *The Great Controversy Theme in E. G. White Writings.* Berrien Springs, Mich.: Andrews University Press, 1978.

Baxter, Richard. *The Saints' Everlasting Rest, or, a Treatise of the Blessed State of the Saints in Their Enjoyment of God in Glory.* London: Thomas Underhill and Francis Taylor, 1652.

Beasley-Murray, G. R. "A Century of Eschatological Discussion." *Expository Times* 64 (1952, 1953): 312-316.

_____. *Jesus and the Future: An Examination of the Criticism of the Eschatological Discourse, Mark 13, With Special Reference to the Little Apocalypse Theory.* London and New York: Macmillan and Co., 1954.

Berkouwer, G. C. *The Return of Christ.* Grand Rapids: Eerdmans, 1972.

Billington, Ray Allen. *The Protestant Crusade, 1800-1860: A Study of the Origins of American Nativism.* New York: Macmillan and Co., 1938.

Blakeley, William Addison, compiler. *Legislative, Executive, Judicial American State Papers Bearing on Sunday Legislation.* New York: National Religious Liberty Association, 1891. Later editions were issued in 1911, 1943, and 1949.

Bliss, Sylvester. "Exposition of the 24th Chapter of Matthew." *Signs of the Time and Expositor of Prophecy*, Nov. 9, 1842, p. 64.

_____. *Memoirs of William Miller, Generally Known as a Lecturer on the Prophecies, and the Second Coming of Christ.* Boston: Joshua V. Himes, 1853. Preface was written by Joshua V. Himes, first three chapters by Elder Apollos Hale.

Boman, Thorleif. *Hebrew Thought Compared With Greek.* New York: W. W. Norton and Co., 1960.

"Books in the E. G. White Library in 1915; On shelves in E. G. White study and in the office and vault (Taken from Ellen G. White Estate Document File 884)." Washington, D.C.: Ellen G. White Estate, n.d. Document File 825.

Bradford, C. E. "How Much Night Left?" *Review and Herald*, July 14, 1975, pp. 14-16.

Bradford, C. E., et al. *Our Times as I See Them.* Nashville: Southern Pub. Assn., 1980.

Branson, Roy. "Adventists Between the Times: The Shift in the Church's Eschatology." *Spectrum*, Winter 1976, pp. 15ff.

Bruner, Frederick Dale. *A Theology of the Holy Spirit; The Pentecostal Experience and the New Testament Witness.* Grand Rapids: Eerdmans, 1970.

Bultmann, Rudolf. "New Testament and Mythology." *Kerygma and Myth.* H. W. Bartsch. New York: Harper and Row, Harper Torchbooks, 1961.

Bunch, Taylor Grant. "The Exodus of Ancient Israel From Ancient Egypt and the Exodus of Modern Israel From Modern Spiritual Babylon." n.p.: by the author, 1937.

Bunyan, John. *The Works of John Bunyan, With an Introduction to Each Treatise, Notes, and a Sketch of His Life, Times, and Contemporaries.* Ed. George Offor. Glasgow: Blackie & Son, 1856. 3 vols. See especially "Of the Resurrection of the Dead," 2: 85-128.

HOW LONG, O LORD?

Clark, Jerome L. *1844: Religious Movements.* Vol. 1; *Social Movements.* Vol. 2; *Intellectual Movements.* Vol. 3. Nashville: Southern Pub. Assn., 1968.

Coffen, Richard W. "John's Apocalypse: Some Second Thoughts on Interpretation." *Spectrum,* Winter 1976, pp. 27ff.

Cottrell, Raymond F. "Ellen G. White's Evaluation and Use of the Bible." *A Symposium on Biblical Hermeneutics.* Edited by Gordon M. Hyde, 1974, pp. 143-161.

_____. "The Eschaton: A Seventh-day Adventist Perspective of the Second Coming." *Spectrum,* vol. 5, No. 1 (1973), pp. 7-31.

Cross, Whitney R. *The Burned-over District: The Social and Intellectual History of Enthusiastic Religion in Western New York, 1800-1850.* New York: Harper & Row, Harper Torchbooks, 1965.

Cullmann, Oscar. *Christ and Time, The Primitive Christian Conception of Time and History.* 3rd ed. London: SCM Press Ltd., 1962.

_____. "Eschatology and Mission in the New Testament." *The Background of the New Testament and Its Eschatology.* Editors W. D. Davies and David Daube. Cambridge: University Press, 1956, pp. 409-421.

_____. *Salvation in History.* London: SCM Press, Ltd., 1967.

Damsteegt, P. Gerard. *Foundations of the Seventh-day Adventist Message and Mission.* Grand Rapids: Eerdmans, 1977.

Dederen, Raoul. "Ellen White's Doctrine of Scripture." *Ministry,* July 1977, pp. 24F-24J.

Delafield, D. A. *Ellen G. White in Europe, 1885-1887: Prepared From Ellen G. White Papers and European Historical Sources.* Washington, D.C.: Review and Herald, 1975.

Dick, Everett N. "William Miller and the Advent Crisis, 1831-1844." Ph.D. dissertation, University of Wisconsin, 1930.

Dodd, C. H. *The Parables of the Kingdom.* London: Nisbet and Co., 1935, Fontana Books, 1961.

Douglass, Herbert E. *The End: Unique Voice of Adventists About the Return of Jesus.* Mountain View, Calif.: Pacific Press, 1979.

_____. *Why Jesus Waits; How the Sanctuary Doctrine Explains the Mission of the Seventh-day Adventist Church.* Washington, D.C.: Review and Herald, 1976.

Douglass, Herbert E., Edward Heppenstall, Hans K. LaRondelle, C. Mervyn Maxwell. *Perfection, the Impossible Possibility.* Nashville: Southern Pub. Assn., 1975.

Edwards, Jonathan. *A History of the Work of Redemption, Containing the Outlines of a Body of Divinity in a Method Entirely New.* New York: Shepard Kollock, for Robert Hodge, 1786.

Fitch, Charles. "'Come Out of Her, My People.'" *Midnight Cry,* Sept. 21, 1843, pp. 33-36.

Froom, Leroy Edwin. *Movement of Destiny.* Washington, D.C.: Review and Herald, 1971.

_____. *The Prophetic Faith of Our Fathers.* Washington, D.C.: Review and Herald, 1950-1954. 4 vols.

Gaustad, Edwin Scott. *The Great Awakening in New England.* New York: Harper and Brothers, 1957.

Hastings, H. L. *The Great Controversy Between God and Man, Its Origin, Progress,*

BIBLIOGRAPHY

and End. Rochester, N.Y.: H. L. Hastings, 1858.

Himes, Joshua V. *Views of the Prophecies and Prophetic Chronology Selected From Manuscripts of William Miller, With a Memoir of His Life*. Boston: Moses A. Dow, 1841.

Johns, Warren L. *Dateline Sunday, U.S.A., The Story of Three and a Half Centuries of Sunday-Law Battles in America*. Mountain View, Calif.: Pacific Press, 1967.

Johnston, Robert Morris. "Parabolic Interpretations Attributed to the Tannaim." Ph.D. dissertation, Hartford Seminary Foundation, June 1977.

Ladd, G. E. *Jesus and the Kingdom: The Eschatology of Biblical Realism*. Waco, Tex.: Word Books, 1964.

Loughborough, J. N. *The Great Second Advent Movement, Its Rise and Progress*. Washington, D.C.: Review and Herald, 1909.

Maxwell, C. Mervyn. "An Exegetical and Historical Examination of the Beginning and Ending of the 1260 Days of Prophecy With Special Attention Given to A.D. 538 and 1798 as Initial and Terminal Dates." M.A. thesis, Seventh-day Adventist Theological Seminary, Washington, D.C., August 1951.

Maxwell, D. M. "The Significance of the Parousia in the Theology of Paul." Ph.D. dissertation, Drew University, 1968.

Miller, William. *Evidences From Scripture and History of the Second Coming of Christ About the Year A.D. 1843 and of His Personal Reign of One Thousand Years*. Brandon, Vt.: Vermont Telegraph Office, 1833.

_____. Letter, Nov. 10, 1844, in *The Midnight Cry*, Dec. 5,1844, pp. 179, 180.

_____. "Synopsis of Miller's Views." *Signs of the Times*, Jan. 25, 1843, pp. 145, 150.

Milton, John. *A Treatise on Christian Doctrine Compiled From the Holy Scriptures Alone*. Translated by Charles R. Sumner. Boston: Cummings, Hilliard, and Co., 1825. 2 volumes.

Neall, Beatrice S. *The Concept of Character in the Apocalypse*. Washington, D.C.: University Press of America, 1983.

Neff, Merlin L. *For God and C.M.E.: A Biography of Percy Magan*. Mountain View, Calif.: Pacific Press, 1964.

Neufeld, Don F. "This Generation Shall Not Pass." *Review and Herald*, Nov. 30, 1972, p. 10; and Apr. 5, 1979, p. 6.

Olson, A. V. *Through Crisis to Victory, 1888-1901*. Washington, D.C.: Review and Herald, 1966. Appendix contains sermons preached by E. G. White at the Minneapolis meeting of the General Conference session in 1888.

Oosterwal, Gottfried. "After 100 Years Why Is the Task of Mission Not Completed?" *Review and Herald*, Jan. 31, 1974, pp. 6-8.

Palmer, Phoebe (Worrell). *Entire Devotion to God*. Salem, Ohio: Schmul Publishers, Rare Reprint Specialists, 1979.

_____. *Full Salvation: Its Doctrine and Duties*. With a memoir of the author by the Rev. I. E. Page. Salem, Ohio: Schmul Publishers, 1979.

Reiber, D. D. "Time-proof Love." *Review and Herald*, Aug. 21, 1975, pp. 8, 9.

Review and Herald Supplement, Aug. 14, 1883.

Schwarz, R. W. *Light Bearers to the Remnant*. Mountain View, Calif.: Pacific Press, 1979.

Schwarzenau, Paul. *Ecumenical Review*, April 1972, pp. 201, 202.

Schweitzer, Albert. *The Quest of the Historical Jesus, a Critical Study of Its Progress*

HOW LONG, O LORD?

From Reimarus to Wrede. New York: Macmillan, 1948.

Talmud, Babylonian. Ed. I. Epstein. London: Soncino Press, 1935. Seder Nezikin, Sanhedrin 97a. b. contains the speculations about when the Messiah would come.

Wesley, John. *The Works of the Rev. John Wesley.* London: Wesleyan Methodist Book Room, 1831. 14 vols. The 3rd ed., published in 1872, was reprinted in 1979 by Baker Book House, Grand Rapids, Mich.

West, Nathaniel, Comp. *Second Coming of Christ: Pre-Millennial Essays of the Prophetic Conference, Held in the Church of the Holy Trinity, New York City.* New York: Fleming H. Revell, 1879.

White, James. "The Prophetic Conference." *Review and Herald,* Feb. 6, 1879, quoting the *Sabbath Recorder* of Dec. 5, 1878, for its information on the prophetic Bible Conference held in New York in 1878. Author's name not listed, but it is likely that it was James White, the editor.

White, James, Ellen G. White and Joseph Bates. *A Word to the "Little Flock."* Brunswick, Maine: James White, 1847.

Wilcox, Francis McLellan. *The Testimony of Jesus, A Review of the Work and Teachings of Mrs. Ellen Gould White.* Washington, D.C.: Review and Herald, 1934.

Wilson, Neal C. "This I Believe About Ellen G. White." *Review and Herald,* Mar. 20, 1980, pp. 8-10.

NOTES

NOTES

NOTES